LIVERPOOL!
THE COMIC STRIP HISTORY

BY BOB BOND

VSP

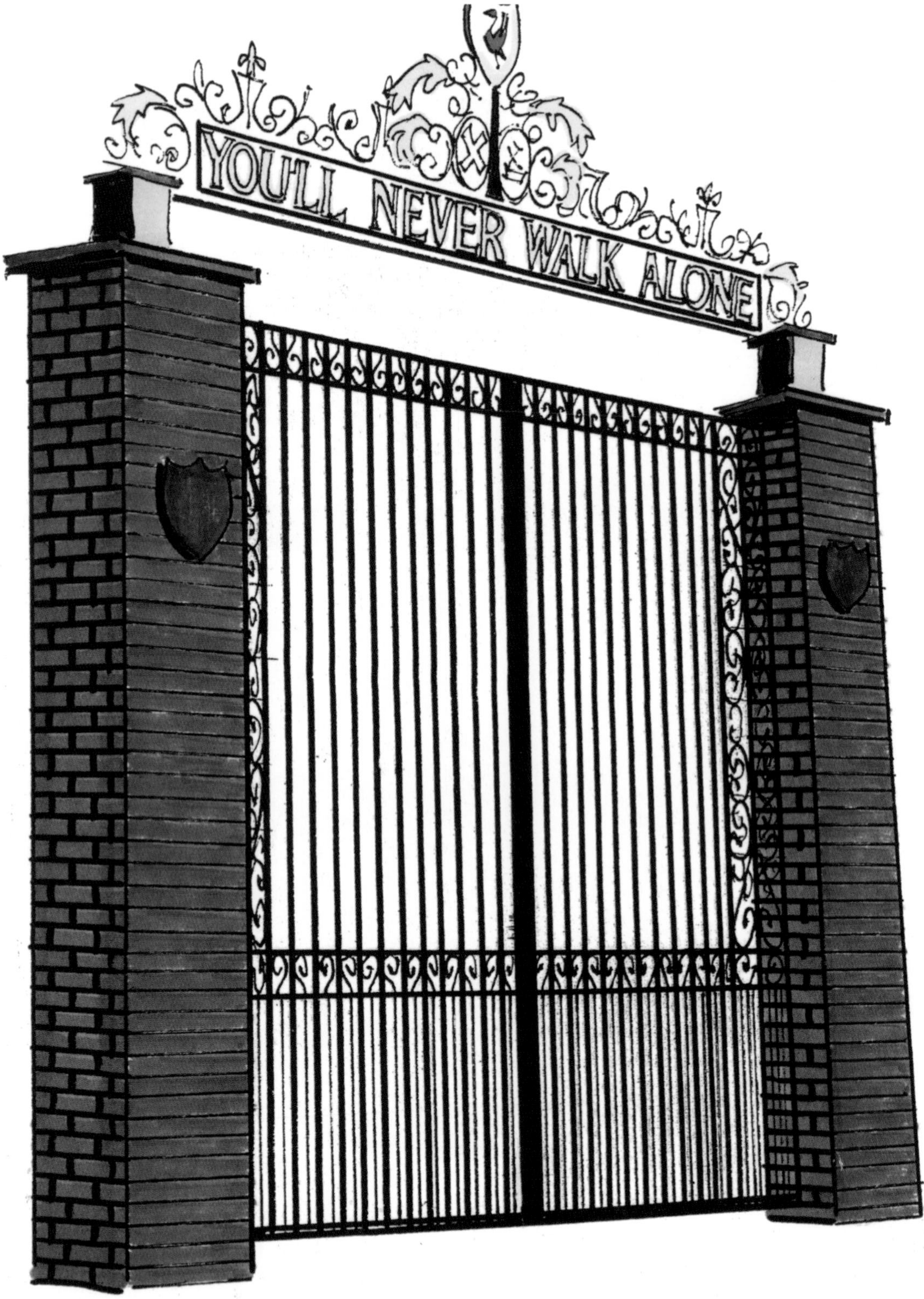
YOU'LL NEVER WALK ALONE

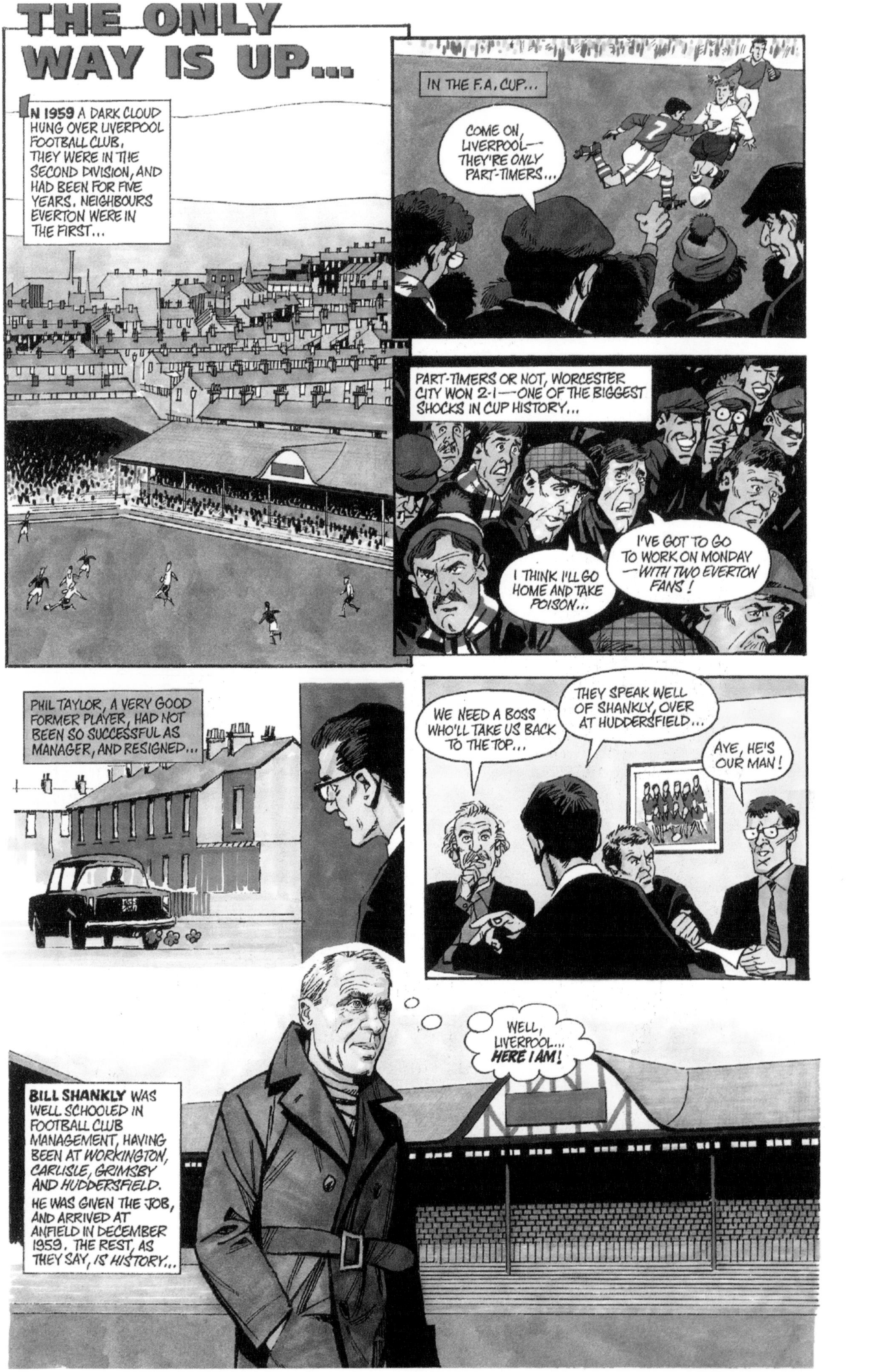
THE ONLY WAY IS UP...
IN 1959 A DARK CLOUD HUNG OVER LIVERPOOL FOOTBALL CLUB. THEY WERE IN THE SECOND DIVISION, AND HAD BEEN FOR FIVE YEARS. NEIGHBOURS EVERTON WERE IN THE FIRST...
IN THE F.A. CUP...
COME ON, LIVERPOOL— THEY'RE ONLY PART-TIMERS...
PART-TIMERS OR NOT, WORCESTER CITY WON 2-1—ONE OF THE BIGGEST SHOCKS IN CUP HISTORY...
I THINK I'LL GO HOME AND TAKE POISON...
I'VE GOT TO GO TO WORK ON MONDAY —WITH TWO EVERTON FANS!
PHIL TAYLOR, A VERY GOOD FORMER PLAYER, HAD NOT BEEN SO SUCCESSFUL AS MANAGER, AND RESIGNED...
WE NEED A BOSS WHO'LL TAKE US BACK TO THE TOP...
THEY SPEAK WELL OF SHANKLY, OVER AT HUDDERSFIELD...
AYE, HE'S OUR MAN!
WELL, LIVERPOOL... HERE I AM!
BILL SHANKLY WAS WELL SCHOOLED IN FOOTBALL CLUB MANAGEMENT, HAVING BEEN AT WORKINGTON, CARLISLE, GRIMSBY AND HUDDERSFIELD.
HE WAS GIVEN THE JOB, AND ARRIVED AT ANFIELD IN DECEMBER 1959. THE REST, AS THEY SAY, IS HISTORY...

FIRST LEAGUE TITLE...

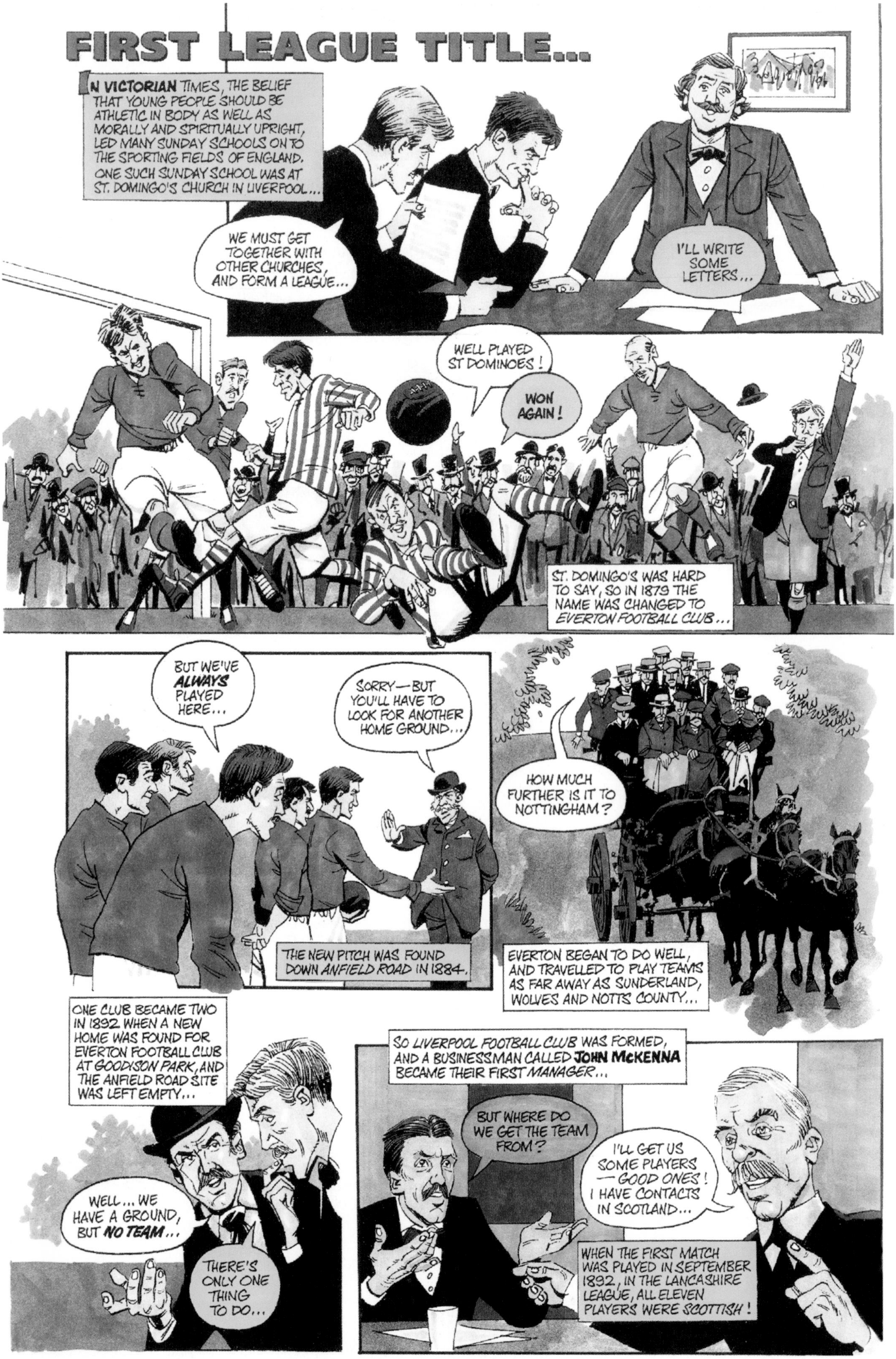
IN VICTORIAN TIMES, THE BELIEF THAT YOUNG PEOPLE SHOULD BE ATHLETIC IN BODY AS WELL AS MORALLY AND SPIRITUALLY UPRIGHT, LED MANY SUNDAY SCHOOLS ON TO THE SPORTING FIELDS OF ENGLAND. ONE SUCH SUNDAY SCHOOL WAS AT ST. DOMINGO'S CHURCH IN LIVERPOOL...
WE MUST GET TOGETHER WITH OTHER CHURCHES, AND FORM A LEAGUE...
I'LL WRITE SOME LETTERS...
WELL PLAYED ST DOMINOES!
WON AGAIN!
ST. DOMINGO'S WAS HARD TO SAY, SO IN 1879 THE NAME WAS CHANGED TO EVERTON FOOTBALL CLUB...
BUT WE'VE ALWAYS PLAYED HERE...
SORRY—BUT YOU'LL HAVE TO LOOK FOR ANOTHER HOME GROUND...
THE NEW PITCH WAS FOUND DOWN ANFIELD ROAD IN 1884.
HOW MUCH FURTHER IS IT TO NOTTINGHAM?
EVERTON BEGAN TO DO WELL, AND TRAVELLED TO PLAY TEAMS AS FAR AWAY AS SUNDERLAND, WOLVES AND NOTTS COUNTY...
ONE CLUB BECAME TWO IN 1892 WHEN A NEW HOME WAS FOUND FOR EVERTON FOOTBALL CLUB AT GOODISON PARK, AND THE ANFIELD ROAD SITE WAS LEFT EMPTY...
WELL... WE HAVE A GROUND, BUT NO TEAM...
THERE'S ONLY ONE THING TO DO...
SO LIVERPOOL FOOTBALL CLUB WAS FORMED, AND A BUSINESSMAN CALLED JOHN McKENNA BECAME THEIR FIRST MANAGER...
BUT WHERE DO WE GET THE TEAM FROM?
I'LL GET US SOME PLAYERS —GOOD ONES! I HAVE CONTACTS IN SCOTLAND...
WHEN THE FIRST MATCH WAS PLAYED IN SEPTEMBER 1892, IN THE LANCASHIRE LEAGUE, ALL ELEVEN PLAYERS WERE SCOTTISH!

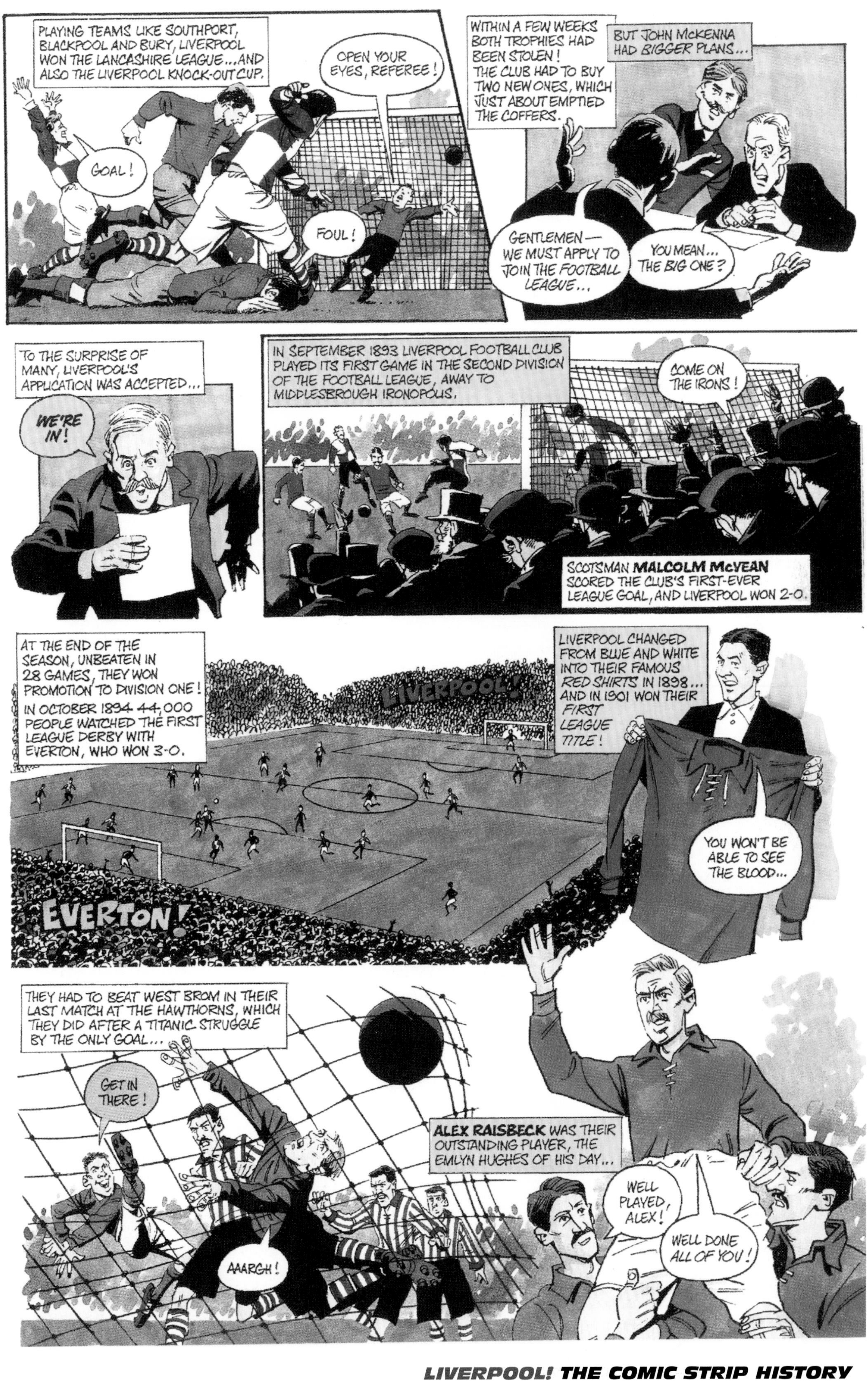

PLAYING TEAMS LIKE SOUTHPORT, BLACKPOOL AND BURY, LIVERPOOL WON THE LANCASHIRE LEAGUE ... AND ALSO THE LIVERPOOL KNOCK-OUT CUP.
GOAL!
OPEN YOUR EYES, REFEREE!
FOUL!
WITHIN A FEW WEEKS BOTH TROPHIES HAD BEEN STOLEN! THE CLUB HAD TO BUY TWO NEW ONES, WHICH JUST ABOUT EMPTIED THE COFFERS.
BUT JOHN McKENNA HAD BIGGER PLANS...
GENTLEMEN— WE MUST APPLY TO JOIN THE FOOTBALL LEAGUE...
YOU MEAN... THE BIG ONE?
TO THE SURPRISE OF MANY, LIVERPOOL'S APPLICATION WAS ACCEPTED...
WE'RE IN!
IN SEPTEMBER 1893 LIVERPOOL FOOTBALL CLUB PLAYED ITS FIRST GAME IN THE SECOND DIVISION OF THE FOOTBALL LEAGUE, AWAY TO MIDDLESBROUGH IRONOPOLIS.
COME ON THE IRONS!
SCOTSMAN MALCOLM McVEAN SCORED THE CLUB'S FIRST-EVER LEAGUE GOAL, AND LIVERPOOL WON 2-0.
AT THE END OF THE SEASON, UNBEATEN IN 28 GAMES, THEY WON PROMOTION TO DIVISION ONE!
IN OCTOBER 1894 44,000 PEOPLE WATCHED THE FIRST LEAGUE DERBY WITH EVERTON, WHO WON 3-0.
LIVERPOOL!
EVERTON!
LIVERPOOL CHANGED FROM BLUE AND WHITE INTO THEIR FAMOUS RED SHIRTS IN 1898... AND IN 1901 WON THEIR FIRST LEAGUE TITLE!
YOU WON'T BE ABLE TO SEE THE BLOOD...
THEY HAD TO BEAT WEST BROM IN THEIR LAST MATCH AT THE HAWTHORNS, WHICH THEY DID AFTER A TITANIC STRUGGLE BY THE ONLY GOAL...
GET IN THERE!
AAARGH!
ALEX RAISBECK WAS THEIR OUTSTANDING PLAYER, THE EMLYN HUGHES OF HIS DAY...
WELL PLAYED, ALEX!
WELL DONE ALL OF YOU!

AND THE KING CAME TOO...

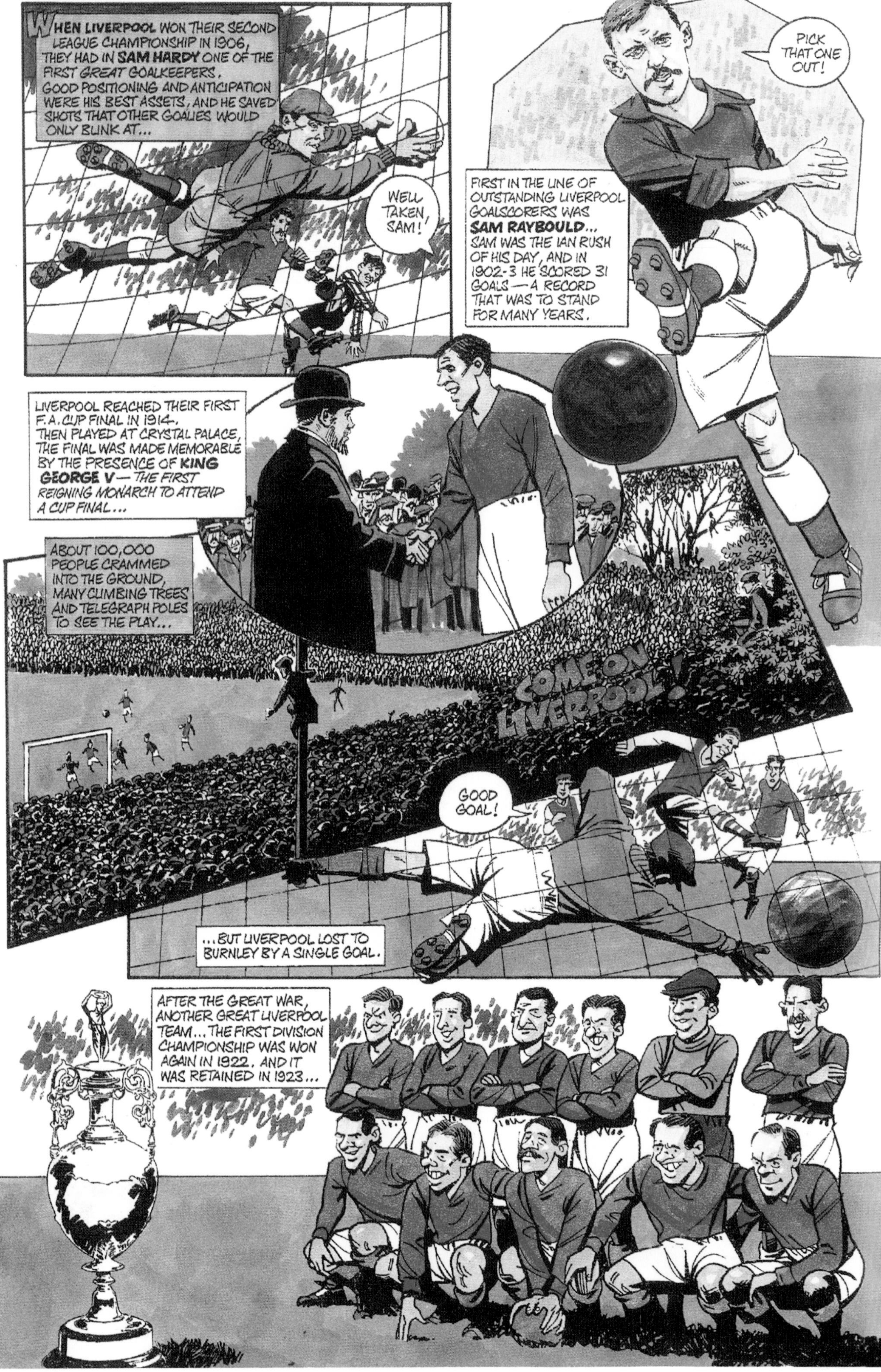

WHEN LIVERPOOL WON THEIR SECOND LEAGUE CHAMPIONSHIP IN 1906, THEY HAD IN SAM HARDY ONE OF THE FIRST GREAT GOALKEEPERS. GOOD POSITIONING AND ANTICIPATION WERE HIS BEST ASSETS, AND HE SAVED SHOTS THAT OTHER GOALIES WOULD ONLY BLINK AT...
WELL TAKEN, SAM!
PICK THAT ONE OUT!
FIRST IN THE LINE OF OUTSTANDING LIVERPOOL GOALSCORERS WAS SAM RAYBOULD... SAM WAS THE IAN RUSH OF HIS DAY, AND IN 1902-3 HE SCORED 31 GOALS — A RECORD THAT WAS TO STAND FOR MANY YEARS.
LIVERPOOL REACHED THEIR FIRST F.A. CUP FINAL IN 1914. THEN PLAYED AT CRYSTAL PALACE, THE FINAL WAS MADE MEMORABLE BY THE PRESENCE OF KING GEORGE V — THE FIRST REIGNING MONARCH TO ATTEND A CUP FINAL...
ABOUT 100,000 PEOPLE CRAMMED INTO THE GROUND, MANY CLIMBING TREES AND TELEGRAPH POLES TO SEE THE PLAY...
COME ON LIVERPOOL!
GOOD GOAL!
...BUT LIVERPOOL LOST TO BURNLEY BY A SINGLE GOAL.
AFTER THE GREAT WAR, ANOTHER GREAT LIVERPOOL TEAM... THE FIRST DIVISION CHAMPIONSHIP WAS WON AGAIN IN 1922, AND IT WAS RETAINED IN 1923...

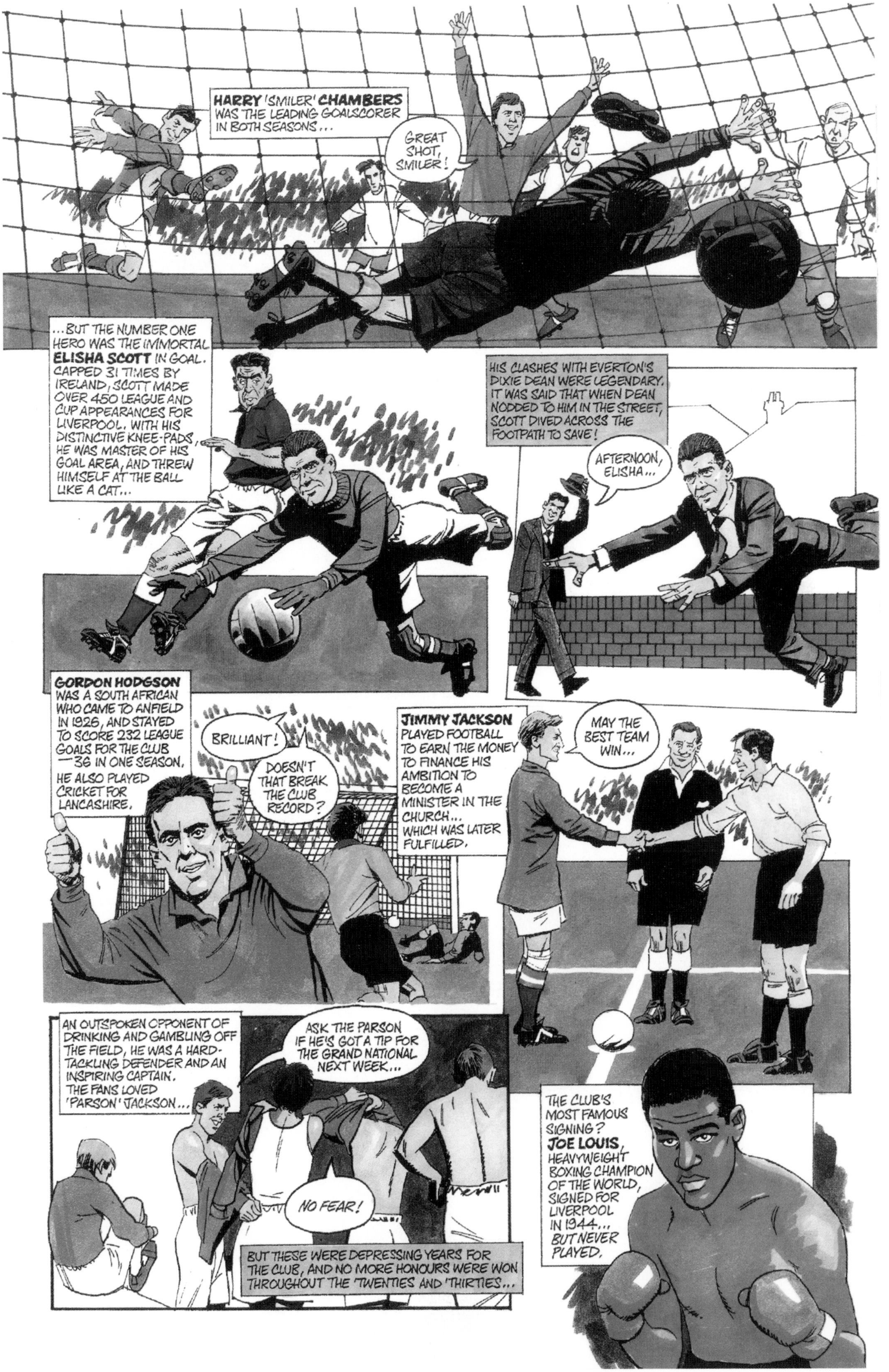
HARRY 'SMILER' CHAMBERS WAS THE LEADING GOALSCORER IN BOTH SEASONS...
GREAT SHOT, SMILER!
...BUT THE NUMBER ONE HERO WAS THE IMMORTAL ELISHA SCOTT IN GOAL. CAPPED 31 TIMES BY IRELAND, SCOTT MADE OVER 450 LEAGUE AND CUP APPEARANCES FOR LIVERPOOL. WITH HIS DISTINCTIVE KNEE-PADS, HE WAS MASTER OF HIS GOAL AREA, AND THREW HIMSELF AT THE BALL LIKE A CAT...
HIS CLASHES WITH EVERTON'S DIXIE DEAN WERE LEGENDARY. IT WAS SAID THAT WHEN DEAN NODDED TO HIM IN THE STREET, SCOTT DIVED ACROSS THE FOOTPATH TO SAVE!
AFTERNOON, ELISHA...
GORDON HODGSON WAS A SOUTH AFRICAN WHO CAME TO ANFIELD IN 1926, AND STAYED TO SCORE 232 LEAGUE GOALS FOR THE CLUB — 36 IN ONE SEASON.
HE ALSO PLAYED CRICKET FOR LANCASHIRE.
BRILLIANT!
DOESN'T THAT BREAK THE CLUB RECORD?
JIMMY JACKSON PLAYED FOOTBALL TO EARN THE MONEY TO FINANCE HIS AMBITION TO BECOME A MINISTER IN THE CHURCH... WHICH WAS LATER FULFILLED.
MAY THE BEST TEAM WIN...
AN OUTSPOKEN OPPONENT OF DRINKING AND GAMBLING OFF THE FIELD, HE WAS A HARD-TACKLING DEFENDER AND AN INSPIRING CAPTAIN. THE FANS LOVED 'PARSON' JACKSON...
ASK THE PARSON IF HE'S GOT A TIP FOR THE GRAND NATIONAL NEXT WEEK...
NO FEAR!
BUT THESE WERE DEPRESSING YEARS FOR THE CLUB, AND NO MORE HONOURS WERE WON THROUGHOUT THE 'TWENTIES AND 'THIRTIES...
THE CLUB'S MOST FAMOUS SIGNING? JOE LOUIS, HEAVYWEIGHT BOXING CHAMPION OF THE WORLD, SIGNED FOR LIVERPOOL IN 1944... BUT NEVER PLAYED.

COME ON LIDDELLPOOL!

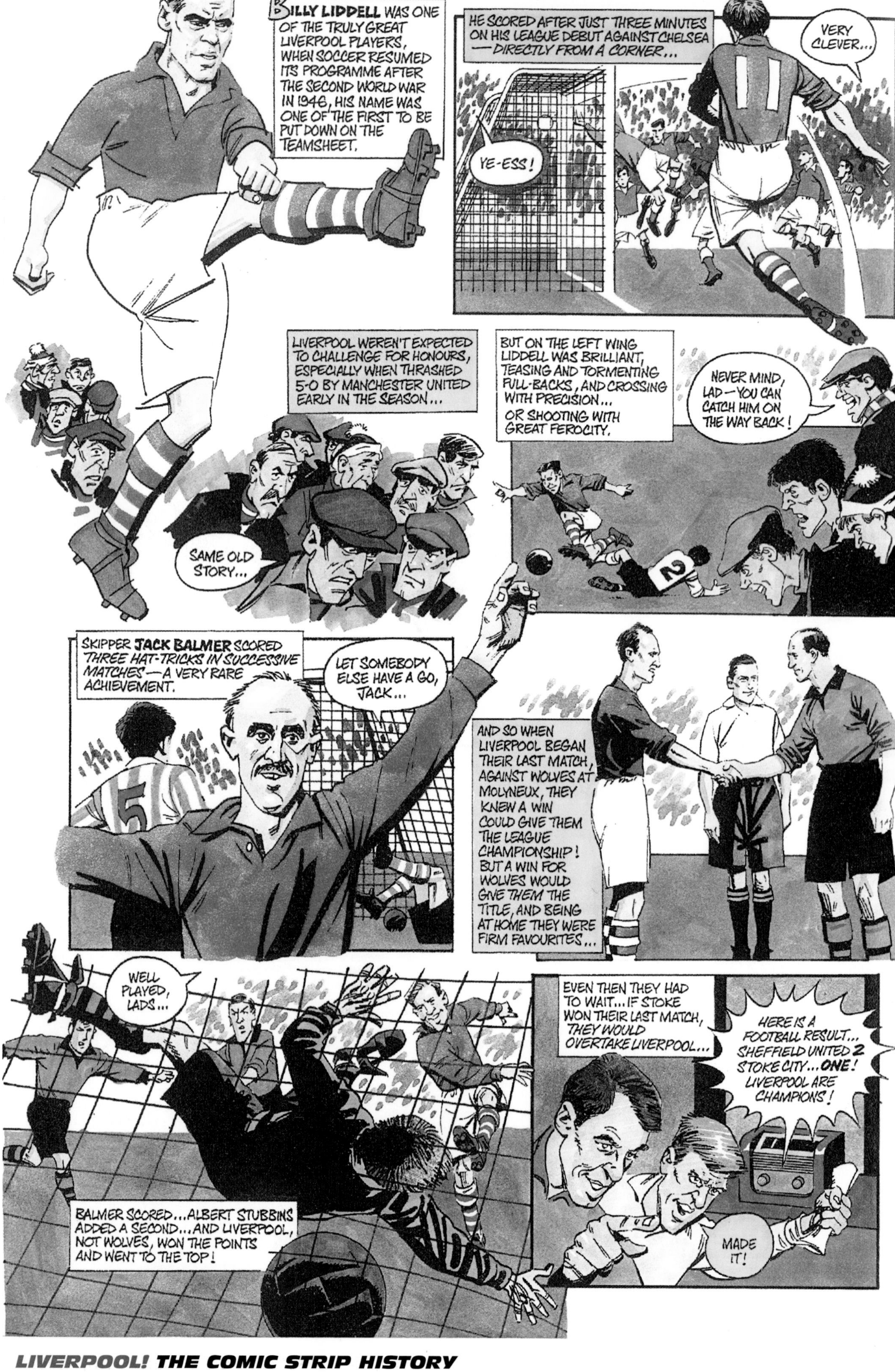
BILLY LIDDELL WAS ONE OF THE TRULY GREAT LIVERPOOL PLAYERS, WHEN SOCCER RESUMED ITS PROGRAMME AFTER THE SECOND WORLD WAR IN 1946, HIS NAME WAS ONE OF THE FIRST TO BE PUT DOWN ON THE TEAMSHEET.
HE SCORED AFTER JUST THREE MINUTES ON HIS LEAGUE DEBUT AGAINST CHELSEA — DIRECTLY FROM A CORNER...
VERY CLEVER...
YE-ESS!
LIVERPOOL WEREN'T EXPECTED TO CHALLENGE FOR HONOURS, ESPECIALLY WHEN THRASHED 5-0 BY MANCHESTER UNITED EARLY IN THE SEASON...
SAME OLD STORY...
BUT ON THE LEFT WING LIDDELL WAS BRILLIANT, TEASING AND TORMENTING FULL-BACKS, AND CROSSING WITH PRECISION...
OR SHOOTING WITH GREAT FEROCITY.
NEVER MIND, LAD — YOU CAN CATCH HIM ON THE WAY BACK!
SKIPPER JACK BALMER SCORED THREE HAT-TRICKS IN SUCCESSIVE MATCHES — A VERY RARE ACHIEVEMENT.
LET SOMEBODY ELSE HAVE A GO, JACK...
AND SO WHEN LIVERPOOL BEGAN THEIR LAST MATCH, AGAINST WOLVES AT MOLYNEUX, THEY KNEW A WIN COULD GIVE THEM THE LEAGUE CHAMPIONSHIP! BUT A WIN FOR WOLVES WOULD GIVE THEM THE TITLE, AND BEING AT HOME THEY WERE FIRM FAVOURITES...
WELL PLAYED, LADS...
BALMER SCORED... ALBERT STUBBINS ADDED A SECOND... AND LIVERPOOL, NOT WOLVES, WON THE POINTS AND WENT TO THE TOP!
EVEN THEN THEY HAD TO WAIT... IF STOKE WON THEIR LAST MATCH, THEY WOULD OVERTAKE LIVERPOOL...
HERE IS A FOOTBALL RESULT... SHEFFIELD UNITED 2 STOKE CITY... ONE! LIVERPOOL ARE CHAMPIONS!
MADE IT!

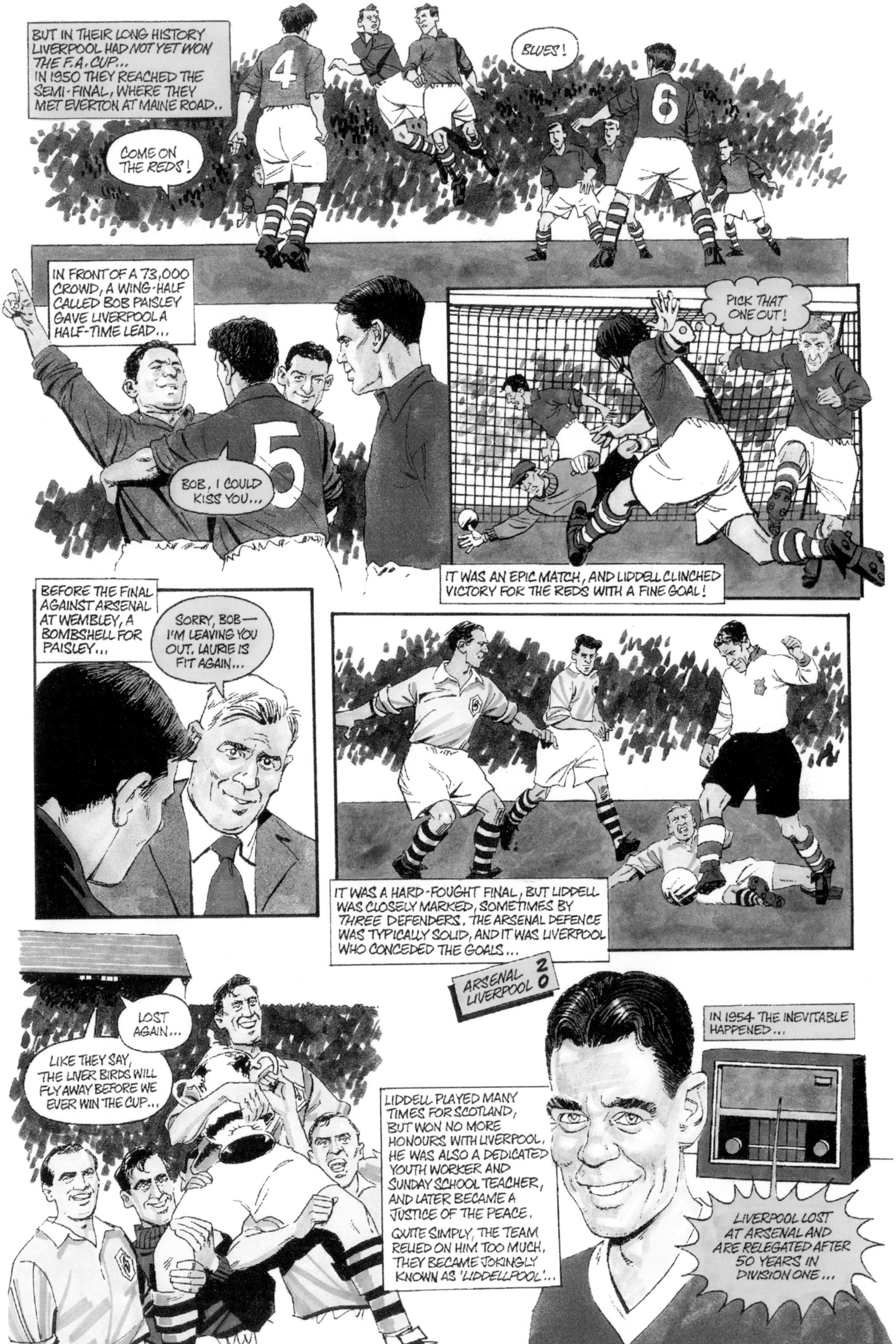
BUT IN THEIR LONG HISTORY LIVERPOOL HAD NOT YET WON THE F.A. CUP...
IN 1950 THEY REACHED THE SEMI-FINAL, WHERE THEY MET EVERTON AT MAINE ROAD..
BLUES!
COME ON THE REDS!
IN FRONT OF A 73,000 CROWD, A WING-HALF CALLED BOB PAISLEY GAVE LIVERPOOL A HALF-TIME LEAD...
BOB, I COULD KISS YOU...
PICK THAT ONE OUT!
IT WAS AN EPIC MATCH, AND LIDDELL CLINCHED VICTORY FOR THE REDS WITH A FINE GOAL!
BEFORE THE FINAL AGAINST ARSENAL AT WEMBLEY, A BOMBSHELL FOR PAISLEY...
SORRY, BOB— I'M LEAVING YOU OUT. LAURIE IS FIT AGAIN...
IT WAS A HARD-FOUGHT FINAL, BUT LIDDELL WAS CLOSELY MARKED, SOMETIMES BY THREE DEFENDERS. THE ARSENAL DEFENCE WAS TYPICALLY SOLID, AND IT WAS LIVERPOOL WHO CONCEDED THE GOALS...
ARSENAL 2
LIVERPOOL 0
LOST AGAIN...
LIKE THEY SAY, THE LIVER BIRDS WILL FLY AWAY BEFORE WE EVER WIN THE CUP...
LIDDELL PLAYED MANY TIMES FOR SCOTLAND, BUT WON NO MORE HONOURS WITH LIVERPOOL. HE WAS ALSO A DEDICATED YOUTH WORKER AND SUNDAY SCHOOL TEACHER, AND LATER BECAME A JUSTICE OF THE PEACE.
QUITE SIMPLY, THE TEAM RELIED ON HIM TOO MUCH. THEY BECAME JOKINGLY KNOWN AS 'LIDDELLPOOL'...
IN 1954 THE INEVITABLE HAPPENED...
LIVERPOOL LOST AT ARSENAL AND ARE RELEGATED AFTER 50 YEARS IN DIVISION ONE...

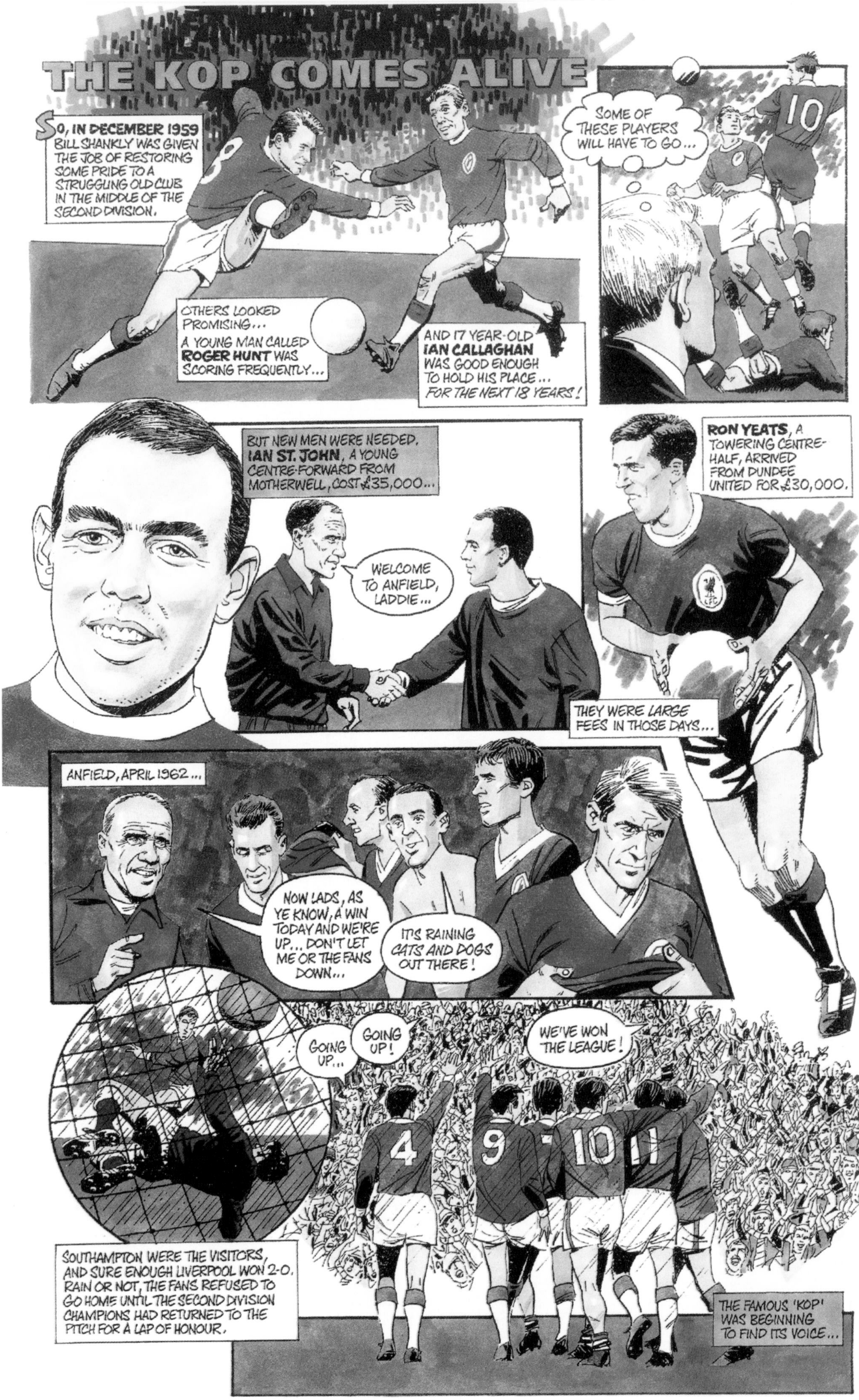
THE KOP COMES ALIVE
SO, IN DECEMBER 1959 BILL SHANKLY WAS GIVEN THE JOB OF RESTORING SOME PRIDE TO A STRUGGLING OLD CLUB IN THE MIDDLE OF THE SECOND DIVISION.
SOME OF THESE PLAYERS WILL HAVE TO GO...
OTHERS LOOKED PROMISING...
A YOUNG MAN CALLED ROGER HUNT WAS SCORING FREQUENTLY...
AND 17 YEAR-OLD IAN CALLAGHAN WAS GOOD ENOUGH TO HOLD HIS PLACE... FOR THE NEXT 18 YEARS!
BUT NEW MEN WERE NEEDED. IAN ST. JOHN, A YOUNG CENTRE-FORWARD FROM MOTHERWELL, COST £35,000...
WELCOME TO ANFIELD, LADDIE...
RON YEATS, A TOWERING CENTRE-HALF, ARRIVED FROM DUNDEE UNITED FOR £30,000.
THEY WERE LARGE FEES IN THOSE DAYS...
ANFIELD, APRIL 1962...
NOW LADS, AS YE KNOW, A WIN TODAY AND WE'RE UP... DON'T LET ME OR THE FANS DOWN...
IT'S RAINING CATS AND DOGS OUT THERE!
GOING UP...
GOING UP!
WE'VE WON THE LEAGUE!
SOUTHAMPTON WERE THE VISITORS, AND SURE ENOUGH LIVERPOOL WON 2-0. RAIN OR NOT, THE FANS REFUSED TO GO HOME UNTIL THE SECOND DIVISION CHAMPIONS HAD RETURNED TO THE PITCH FOR A LAP OF HONOUR.
THE FAMOUS 'KOP' WAS BEGINNING TO FIND ITS VOICE...

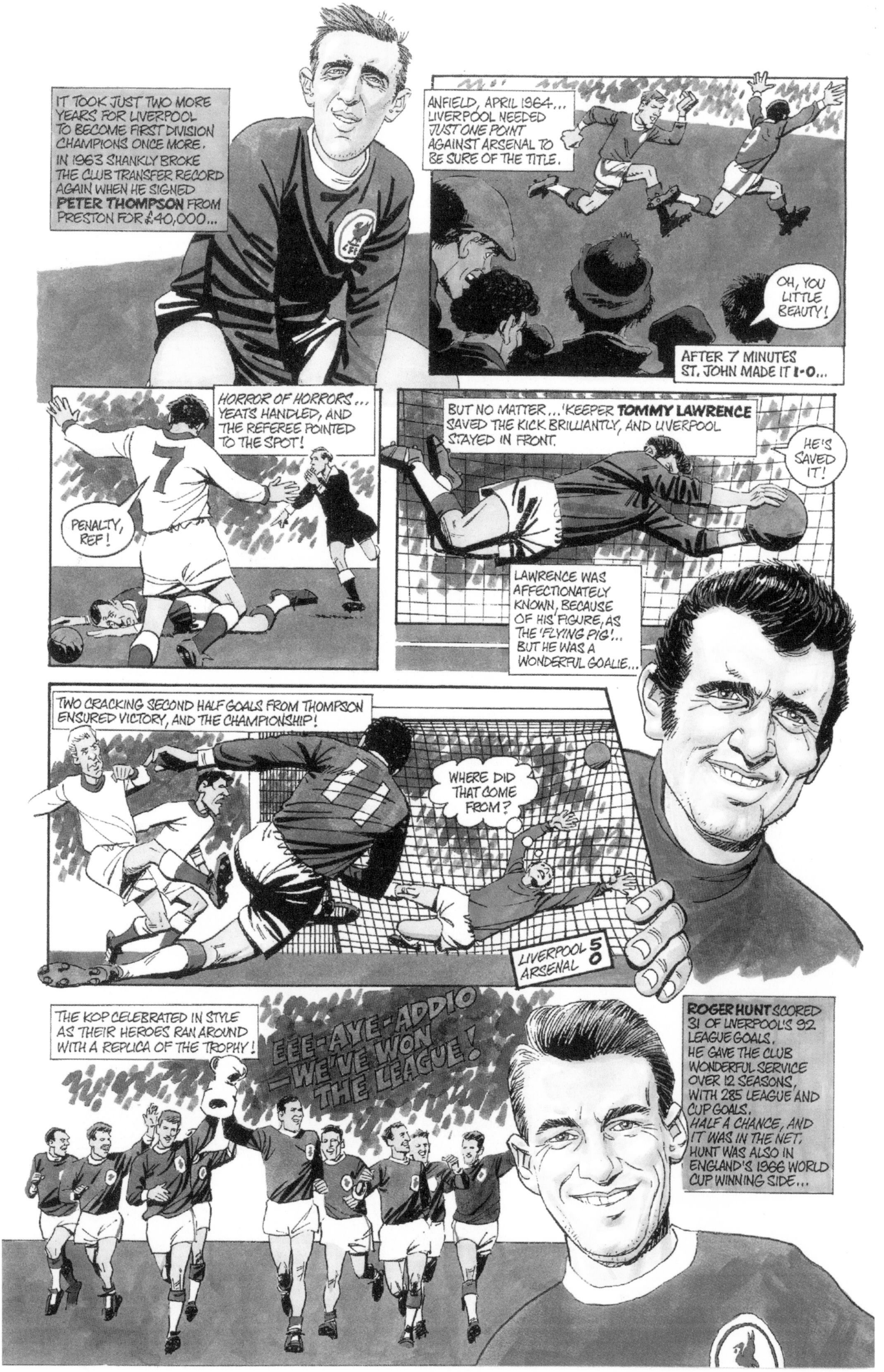
IT TOOK JUST TWO MORE YEARS FOR LIVERPOOL TO BECOME FIRST DIVISION CHAMPIONS ONCE MORE.
IN 1963 SHANKLY BROKE THE CLUB TRANSFER RECORD AGAIN WHEN HE SIGNED **PETER THOMPSON** FROM PRESTON FOR £40,000...
ANFIELD, APRIL 1964... LIVERPOOL NEEDED JUST ONE POINT AGAINST ARSENAL TO BE SURE OF THE TITLE.
OH, YOU LITTLE BEAUTY!
AFTER 7 MINUTES ST. JOHN MADE IT 1-0...
HORROR OF HORRORS... YEATS HANDLED, AND THE REFEREE POINTED TO THE SPOT!
PENALTY, REF!
BUT NO MATTER...'KEEPER **TOMMY LAWRENCE** SAVED THE KICK BRILLIANTLY, AND LIVERPOOL STAYED IN FRONT.
HE'S SAVED IT!
LAWRENCE WAS AFFECTIONATELY KNOWN, BECAUSE OF HIS FIGURE, AS THE 'FLYING PIG'... BUT HE WAS A WONDERFUL GOALIE...
TWO CRACKING SECOND HALF GOALS FROM THOMPSON ENSURED VICTORY, AND THE CHAMPIONSHIP!
WHERE DID THAT COME FROM?
LIVERPOOL 5
ARSENAL 0
THE KOP CELEBRATED IN STYLE AS THEIR HEROES RAN AROUND WITH A REPLICA OF THE TROPHY!
EEE-AYE-ADDIO — WE'VE WON THE LEAGUE!
ROGER HUNT SCORED 31 OF LIVERPOOL'S 92 LEAGUE GOALS. HE GAVE THE CLUB WONDERFUL SERVICE OVER 12 SEASONS, WITH 285 LEAGUE AND CUP GOALS. HALF A CHANCE, AND IT WAS IN THE NET. HUNT WAS ALSO IN ENGLAND'S 1966 WORLD CUP WINNING SIDE...

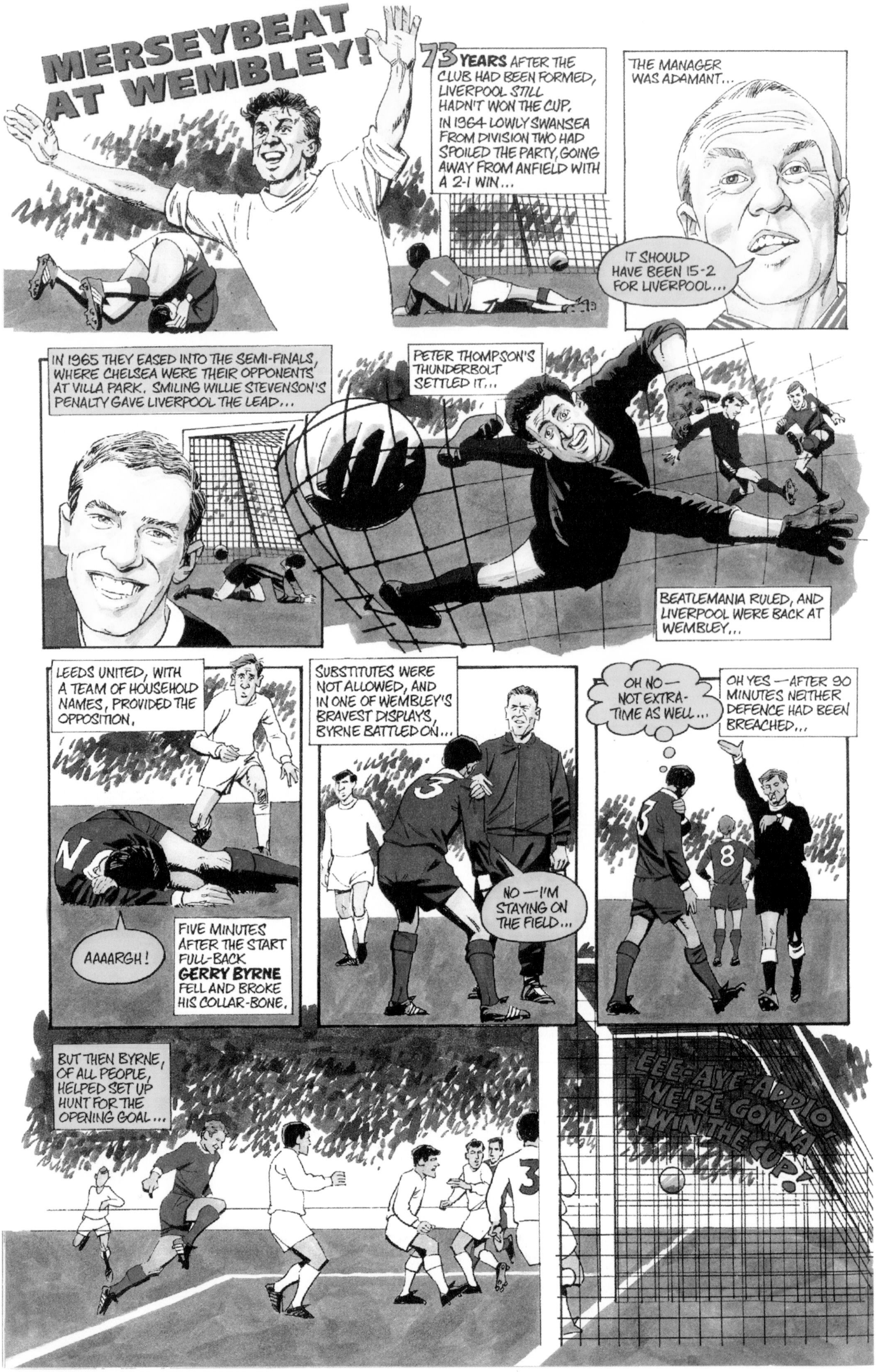
MERSEYBEAT AT WEMBLEY!
73 YEARS AFTER THE CLUB HAD BEEN FORMED, LIVERPOOL STILL HADN'T WON THE CUP. IN 1964 LOWLY SWANSEA FROM DIVISION TWO HAD SPOILED THE PARTY, GOING AWAY FROM ANFIELD WITH A 2-1 WIN...
THE MANAGER WAS ADAMANT...
IT SHOULD HAVE BEEN 15-2 FOR LIVERPOOL...
IN 1965 THEY EASED INTO THE SEMI-FINALS, WHERE CHELSEA WERE THEIR OPPONENTS AT VILLA PARK. SMILING WILLIE STEVENSON'S PENALTY GAVE LIVERPOOL THE LEAD...
PETER THOMPSON'S THUNDERBOLT SETTLED IT...
BEATLEMANIA RULED, AND LIVERPOOL WERE BACK AT WEMBLEY...
LEEDS UNITED, WITH A TEAM OF HOUSEHOLD NAMES, PROVIDED THE OPPOSITION.
AAAARGH!
FIVE MINUTES AFTER THE START FULL-BACK GERRY BYRNE FELL AND BROKE HIS COLLAR-BONE.
SUBSTITUTES WERE NOT ALLOWED, AND IN ONE OF WEMBLEY'S BRAVEST DISPLAYS, BYRNE BATTLED ON...
NO — I'M STAYING ON THE FIELD...
OH NO — NOT EXTRA-TIME AS WELL...
OH YES — AFTER 90 MINUTES NEITHER DEFENCE HAD BEEN BREACHED...
BUT THEN BYRNE, OF ALL PEOPLE, HELPED SET UP HUNT FOR THE OPENING GOAL...
EEE-AYE-ADDIO! WE'RE GONNA WIN THE CUP!

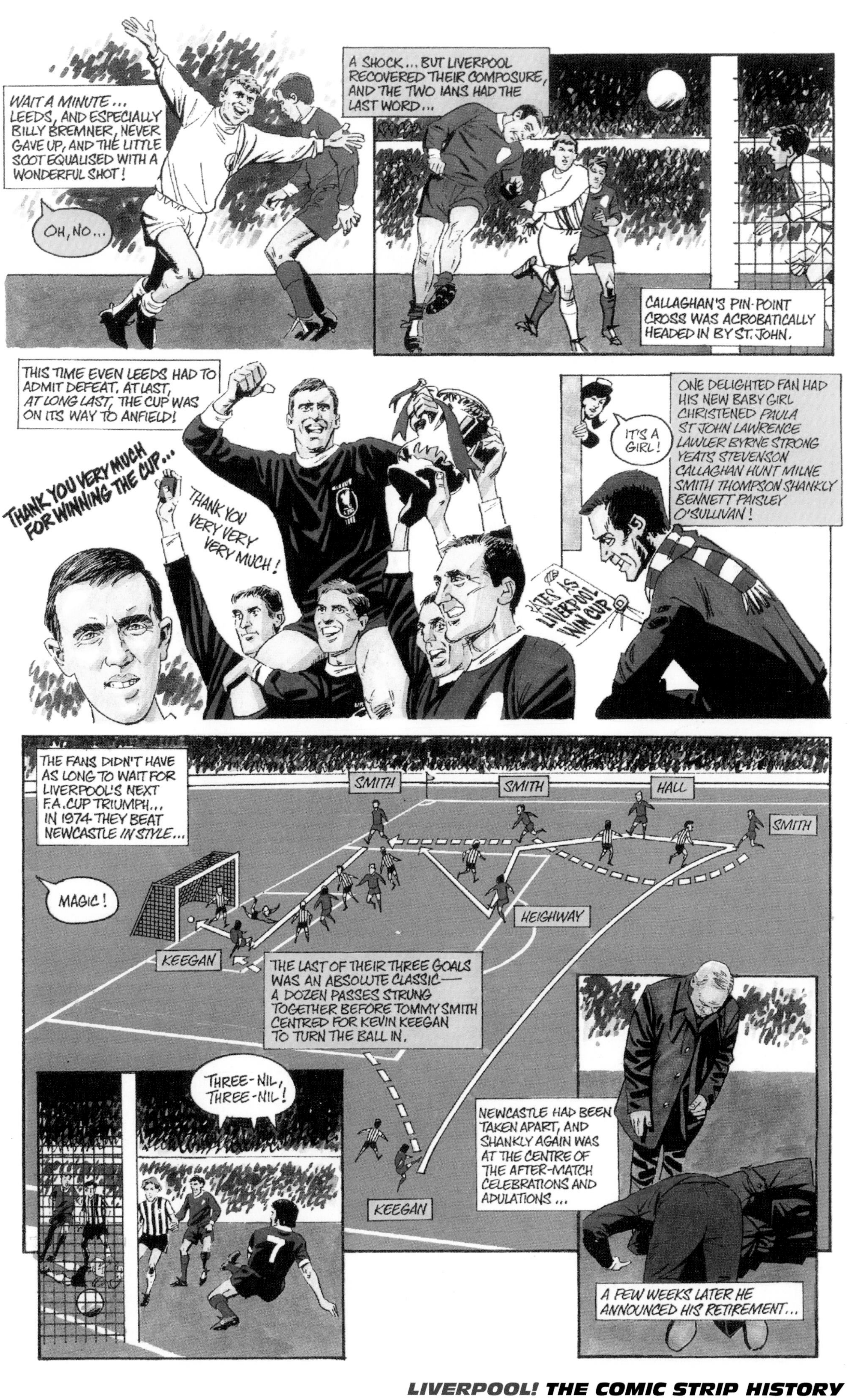
WAIT A MINUTE... LEEDS, AND ESPECIALLY BILLY BREMNER, NEVER GAVE UP, AND THE LITTLE SCOT EQUALISED WITH A WONDERFUL SHOT!
OH, NO...
A SHOCK... BUT LIVERPOOL RECOVERED THEIR COMPOSURE, AND THE TWO IANS HAD THE LAST WORD...
CALLAGHAN'S PIN-POINT CROSS WAS ACROBATICALLY HEADED IN BY ST. JOHN.
THIS TIME EVEN LEEDS HAD TO ADMIT DEFEAT. AT LAST, AT LONG LAST, THE CUP WAS ON ITS WAY TO ANFIELD!
THANK YOU VERY MUCH FOR WINNING THE CUP...
THANK YOU VERY VERY VERY MUCH!
IT'S A GIRL!
ONE DELIGHTED FAN HAD HIS NEW BABY GIRL CHRISTENED PAULA ST JOHN LAWRENCE LAWLER BYRNE STRONG YEATS STEVENSON CALLAGHAN HUNT MILNE SMITH THOMPSON SHANKLY BENNETT PAISLEY O'SULLIVAN!
LATEST LIVERPOOL WIN CUP
THE FANS DIDN'T HAVE AS LONG TO WAIT FOR LIVERPOOL'S NEXT F.A. CUP TRIUMPH... IN 1974 THEY BEAT NEWCASTLE IN STYLE...
SMITH
SMITH
HALL
SMITH
MAGIC!
HEIGHWAY
KEEGAN
THE LAST OF THEIR THREE GOALS WAS AN ABSOLUTE CLASSIC— A DOZEN PASSES STRUNG TOGETHER BEFORE TOMMY SMITH CENTRED FOR KEVIN KEEGAN TO TURN THE BALL IN.
THREE-NIL, THREE-NIL!
KEEGAN
NEWCASTLE HAD BEEN TAKEN APART, AND SHANKLY AGAIN WAS AT THE CENTRE OF THE AFTER-MATCH CELEBRATIONS AND ADULATIONS...
A FEW WEEKS LATER HE ANNOUNCED HIS RETIREMENT...

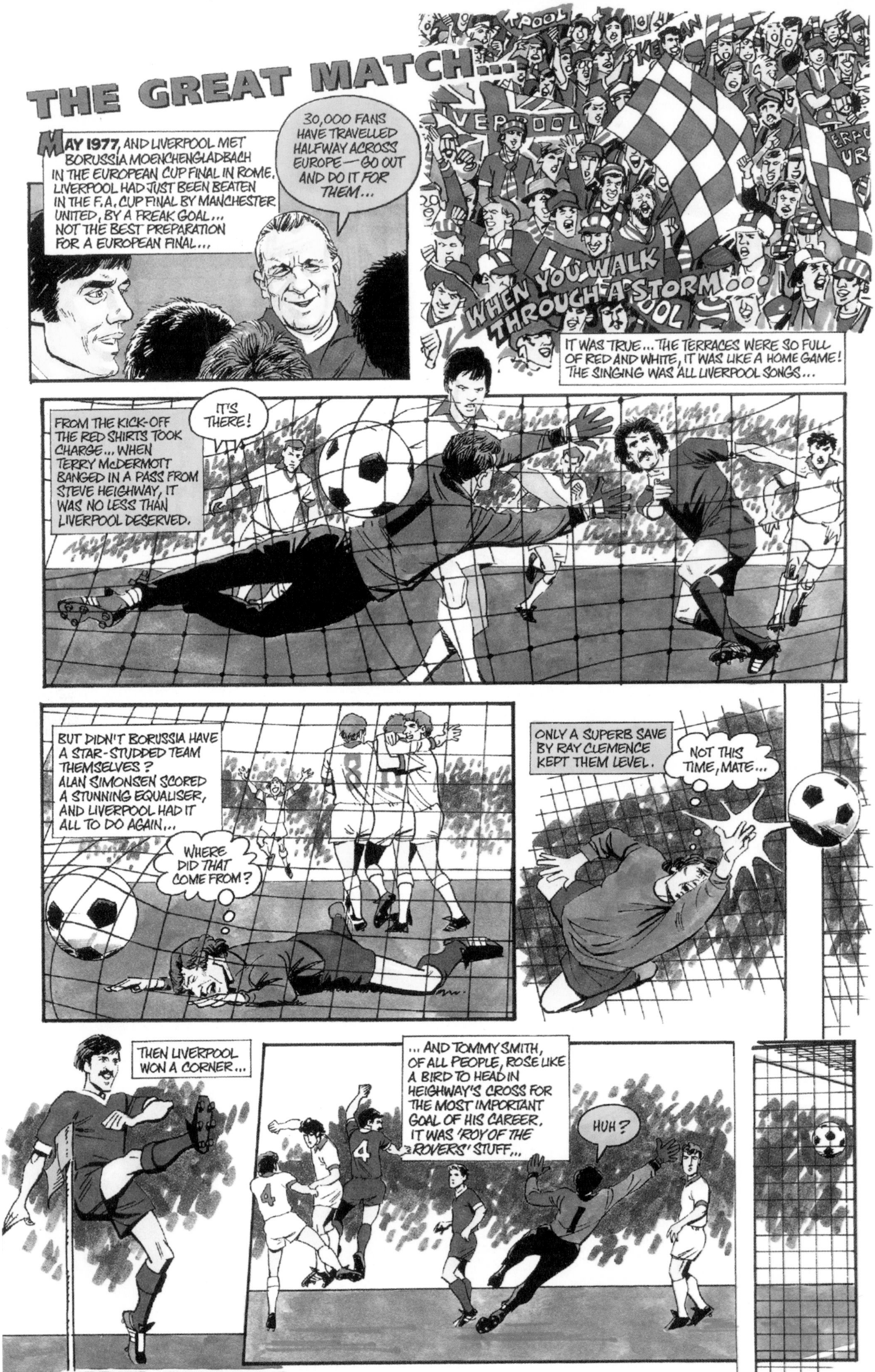
THE GREAT MATCH...
MAY 1977, AND LIVERPOOL MET BORUSSIA MOENCHENGLADBACH IN THE EUROPEAN CUP FINAL IN ROME. LIVERPOOL HAD JUST BEEN BEATEN IN THE F.A. CUP FINAL BY MANCHESTER UNITED, BY A FREAK GOAL... NOT THE BEST PREPARATION FOR A EUROPEAN FINAL...
30,000 FANS HAVE TRAVELLED HALFWAY ACROSS EUROPE — GO OUT AND DO IT FOR THEM...
WHEN YOU WALK THROUGH A STORM...
IT WAS TRUE... THE TERRACES WERE SO FULL OF RED AND WHITE, IT WAS LIKE A HOME GAME! THE SINGING WAS ALL LIVERPOOL SONGS...
FROM THE KICK-OFF THE RED SHIRTS TOOK CHARGE... WHEN TERRY McDERMOTT BANGED IN A PASS FROM STEVE HEIGHWAY, IT WAS NO LESS THAN LIVERPOOL DESERVED.
IT'S THERE!
BUT DIDN'T BORUSSIA HAVE A STAR-STUDDED TEAM THEMSELVES? ALAN SIMONSEN SCORED A STUNNING EQUALISER, AND LIVERPOOL HAD IT ALL TO DO AGAIN...
WHERE DID THAT COME FROM?
ONLY A SUPERB SAVE BY RAY CLEMENCE KEPT THEM LEVEL.
NOT THIS TIME, MATE...
THEN LIVERPOOL WON A CORNER...
... AND TOMMY SMITH, OF ALL PEOPLE, ROSE LIKE A BIRD TO HEAD IN HEIGHWAY'S CROSS FOR THE MOST IMPORTANT GOAL OF HIS CAREER. IT WAS 'ROY OF THE ROVERS' STUFF...
HUH?

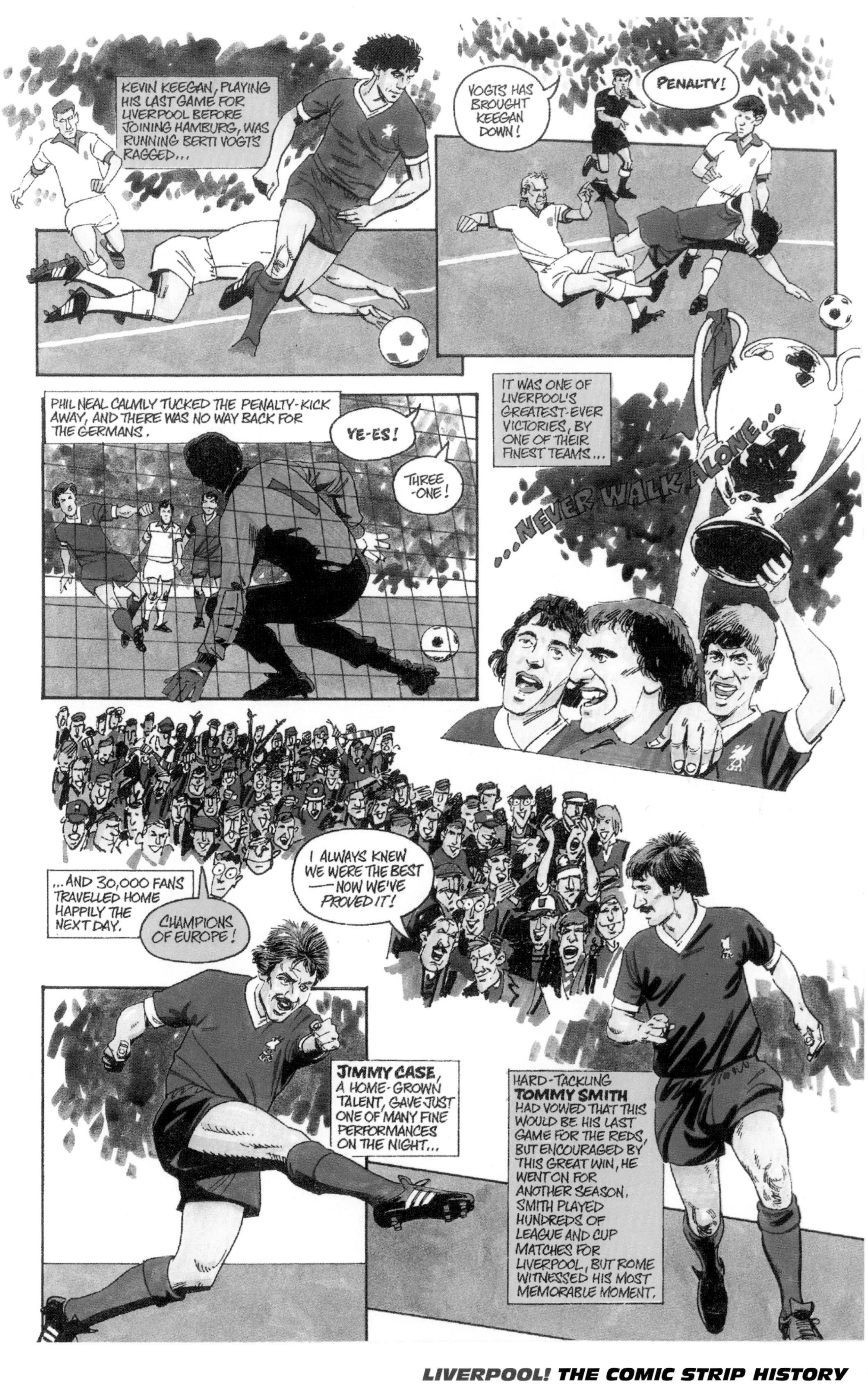
KEVIN KEEGAN, PLAYING HIS LAST GAME FOR LIVERPOOL BEFORE JOINING HAMBURG, WAS RUNNING BERTI VOGTS RAGGED...
VOGTS HAS BROUGHT KEEGAN DOWN!
PENALTY!
PHIL NEAL CALMLY TUCKED THE PENALTY-KICK AWAY, AND THERE WAS NO WAY BACK FOR THE GERMANS.
YE-ES!
THREE -ONE!
IT WAS ONE OF LIVERPOOL'S GREATEST-EVER VICTORIES, BY ONE OF THEIR FINEST TEAMS...
...NEVER WALK ALONE...
...AND 30,000 FANS TRAVELLED HOME HAPPILY THE NEXT DAY.
CHAMPIONS OF EUROPE!
I ALWAYS KNEW WE WERE THE BEST —NOW WE'VE PROVED IT!
JIMMY CASE, A HOME-GROWN TALENT, GAVE JUST ONE OF MANY FINE PERFORMANCES ON THE NIGHT...
HARD-TACKLING TOMMY SMITH HAD VOWED THAT THIS WOULD BE HIS LAST GAME FOR THE REDS, BUT ENCOURAGED BY THIS GREAT WIN, HE WENT ON FOR ANOTHER SEASON. SMITH PLAYED HUNDREDS OF LEAGUE AND CUP MATCHES FOR LIVERPOOL, BUT ROME WITNESSED HIS MOST MEMORABLE MOMENT.

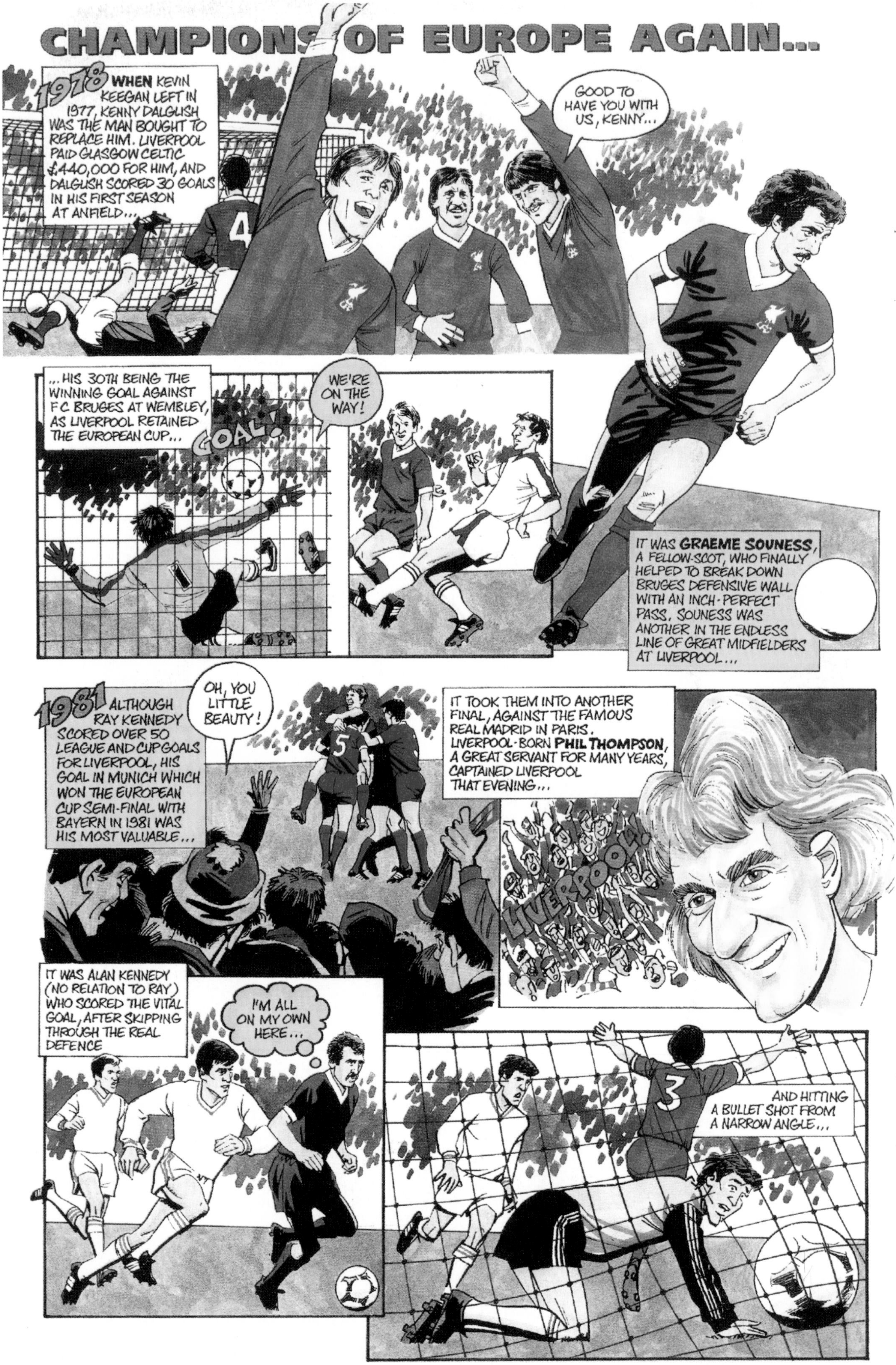
CHAMPIONS OF EUROPE AGAIN...
1978 WHEN KEVIN KEEGAN LEFT IN 1977, KENNY DALGLISH WAS THE MAN BOUGHT TO REPLACE HIM. LIVERPOOL PAID GLASGOW CELTIC £440,000 FOR HIM, AND DALGLISH SCORED 30 GOALS IN HIS FIRST SEASON AT ANFIELD...
GOOD TO HAVE YOU WITH US, KENNY...
...HIS 30TH BEING THE WINNING GOAL AGAINST F.C. BRUGES AT WEMBLEY, AS LIVERPOOL RETAINED THE EUROPEAN CUP...
GOAL!
WE'RE ON THE WAY!
IT WAS GRAEME SOUNESS, A FELLOW-SCOT, WHO FINALLY HELPED TO BREAK DOWN BRUGES DEFENSIVE WALL WITH AN INCH-PERFECT PASS. SOUNESS WAS ANOTHER IN THE ENDLESS LINE OF GREAT MIDFIELDERS AT LIVERPOOL...
1981 ALTHOUGH RAY KENNEDY SCORED OVER 50 LEAGUE AND CUP GOALS FOR LIVERPOOL, HIS GOAL IN MUNICH WHICH WON THE EUROPEAN CUP SEMI-FINAL WITH BAYERN IN 1981 WAS HIS MOST VALUABLE...
OH, YOU LITTLE BEAUTY!
IT TOOK THEM INTO ANOTHER FINAL, AGAINST THE FAMOUS REAL MADRID IN PARIS. LIVERPOOL-BORN PHIL THOMPSON, A GREAT SERVANT FOR MANY YEARS, CAPTAINED LIVERPOOL THAT EVENING...
LIVERPOOL!
IT WAS ALAN KENNEDY (NO RELATION TO RAY) WHO SCORED THE VITAL GOAL, AFTER SKIPPING THROUGH THE REAL DEFENCE
I'M ALL ON MY OWN HERE...
AND HITTING A BULLET SHOT FROM A NARROW ANGLE...

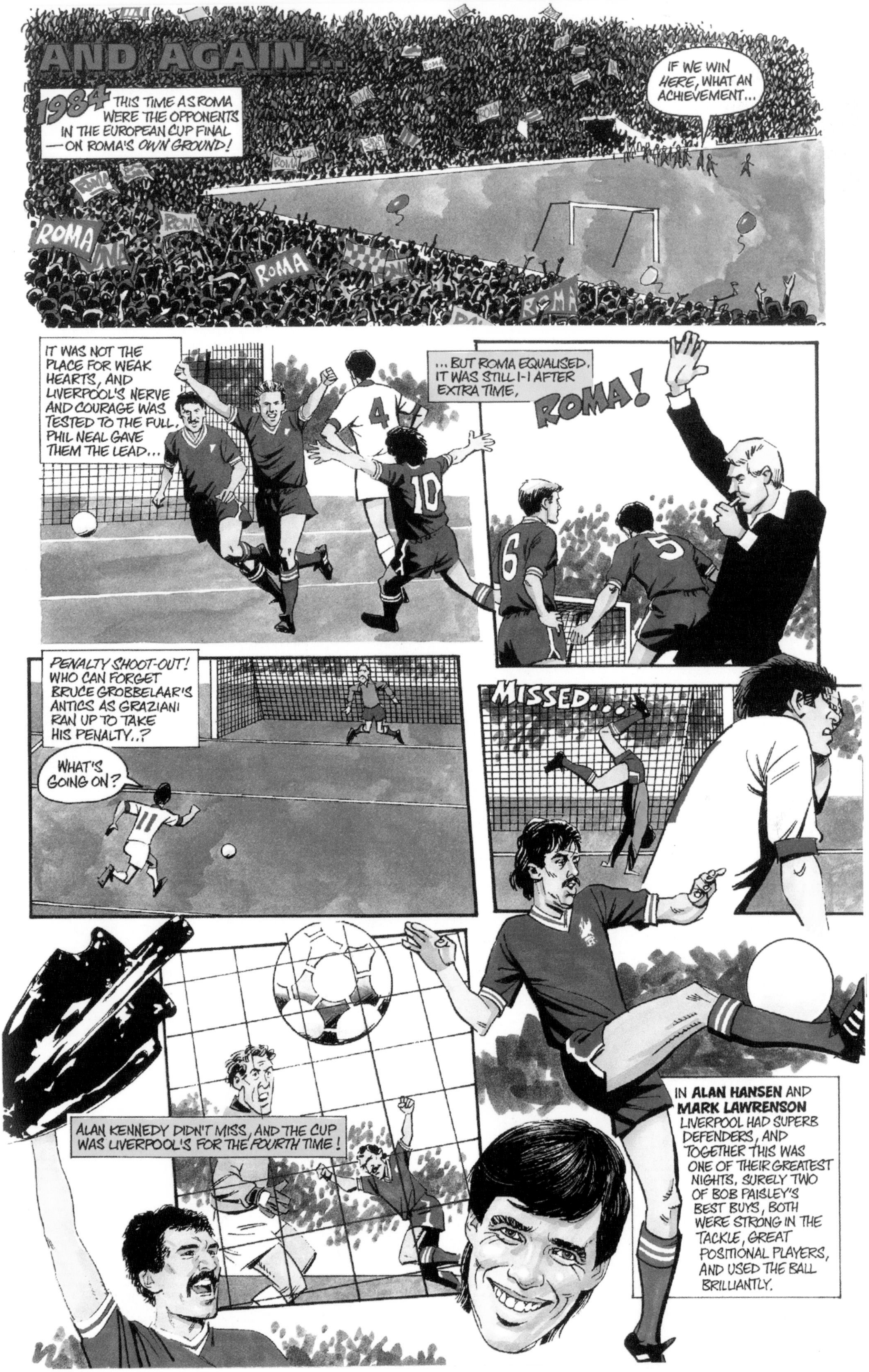
AND AGAIN...
1984 THIS TIME AS ROMA WERE THE OPPONENTS IN THE EUROPEAN CUP FINAL — ON ROMA'S OWN GROUND!
IF WE WIN HERE, WHAT AN ACHIEVEMENT...
ROMA
IT WAS NOT THE PLACE FOR WEAK HEARTS, AND LIVERPOOL'S NERVE AND COURAGE WAS TESTED TO THE FULL. PHIL NEAL GAVE THEM THE LEAD...
...BUT ROMA EQUALISED, IT WAS STILL 1-1 AFTER EXTRA TIME.
ROMA!
PENALTY SHOOT-OUT! WHO CAN FORGET BRUCE GROBBELAAR'S ANTICS AS GRAZIANI RAN UP TO TAKE HIS PENALTY..?
WHAT'S GOING ON?
MISSED...
ALAN KENNEDY DIDN'T MISS, AND THE CUP WAS LIVERPOOL'S FOR THE FOURTH TIME!
IN ALAN HANSEN AND MARK LAWRENSON LIVERPOOL HAD SUPERB DEFENDERS, AND TOGETHER THIS WAS ONE OF THEIR GREATEST NIGHTS, SURELY TWO OF BOB PAISLEY'S BEST BUYS, BOTH WERE STRONG IN THE TACKLE, GREAT POSITIONAL PLAYERS, AND USED THE BALL BRILLIANTLY.

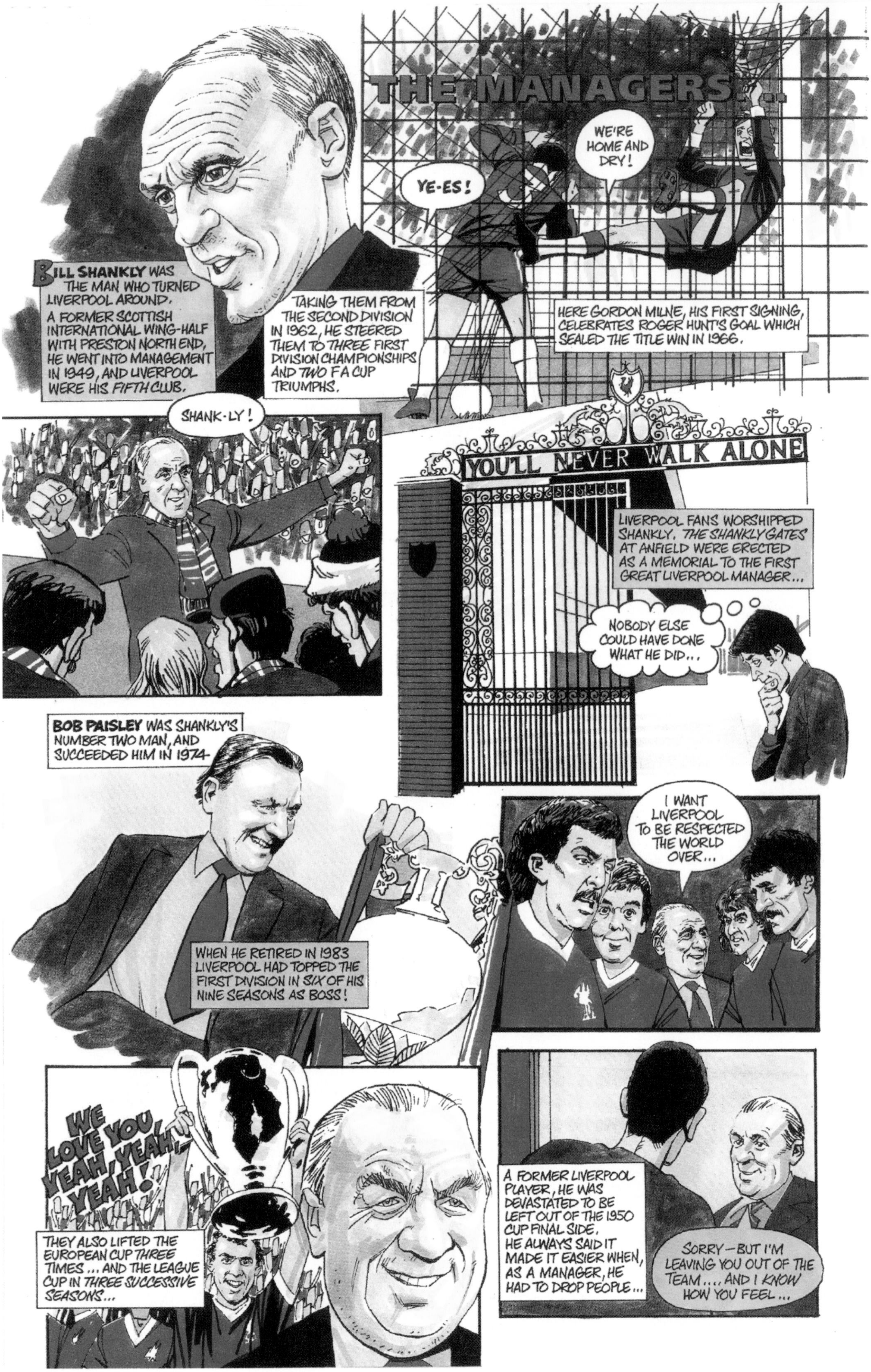
THE MANAGERS...
BILL SHANKLY WAS THE MAN WHO TURNED LIVERPOOL AROUND. A FORMER SCOTTISH INTERNATIONAL WING-HALF WITH PRESTON NORTH END, HE WENT INTO MANAGEMENT IN 1949, AND LIVERPOOL WERE HIS FIFTH CLUB.
TAKING THEM FROM THE SECOND DIVISION IN 1962, HE STEERED THEM TO THREE FIRST DIVISION CHAMPIONSHIPS AND TWO FA CUP TRIUMPHS.
YE-ES!
WE'RE HOME AND DRY!
HERE GORDON MILNE, HIS FIRST SIGNING, CELEBRATES ROGER HUNT'S GOAL WHICH SEALED THE TITLE WIN IN 1966.
SHANK-LY!
YOU'LL NEVER WALK ALONE
LIVERPOOL FANS WORSHIPPED SHANKLY. THE SHANKLY GATES AT ANFIELD WERE ERECTED AS A MEMORIAL TO THE FIRST GREAT LIVERPOOL MANAGER...
NOBODY ELSE COULD HAVE DONE WHAT HE DID...
BOB PAISLEY WAS SHANKLY'S NUMBER TWO MAN, AND SUCCEEDED HIM IN 1974.
I WANT LIVERPOOL TO BE RESPECTED THE WORLD OVER...
WHEN HE RETIRED IN 1983 LIVERPOOL HAD TOPPED THE FIRST DIVISION IN SIX OF HIS NINE SEASONS AS BOSS!
WE LOVE YOU, YEAH, YEAH, YEAH!
THEY ALSO LIFTED THE EUROPEAN CUP THREE TIMES ... AND THE LEAGUE CUP IN THREE SUCCESSIVE SEASONS...
A FORMER LIVERPOOL PLAYER, HE WAS DEVASTATED TO BE LEFT OUT OF THE 1950 CUP FINAL SIDE. HE ALWAYS SAID IT MADE IT EASIER WHEN, AS A MANAGER, HE HAD TO DROP PEOPLE...
SORRY — BUT I'M LEAVING YOU OUT OF THE TEAM..., AND I KNOW HOW YOU FEEL...

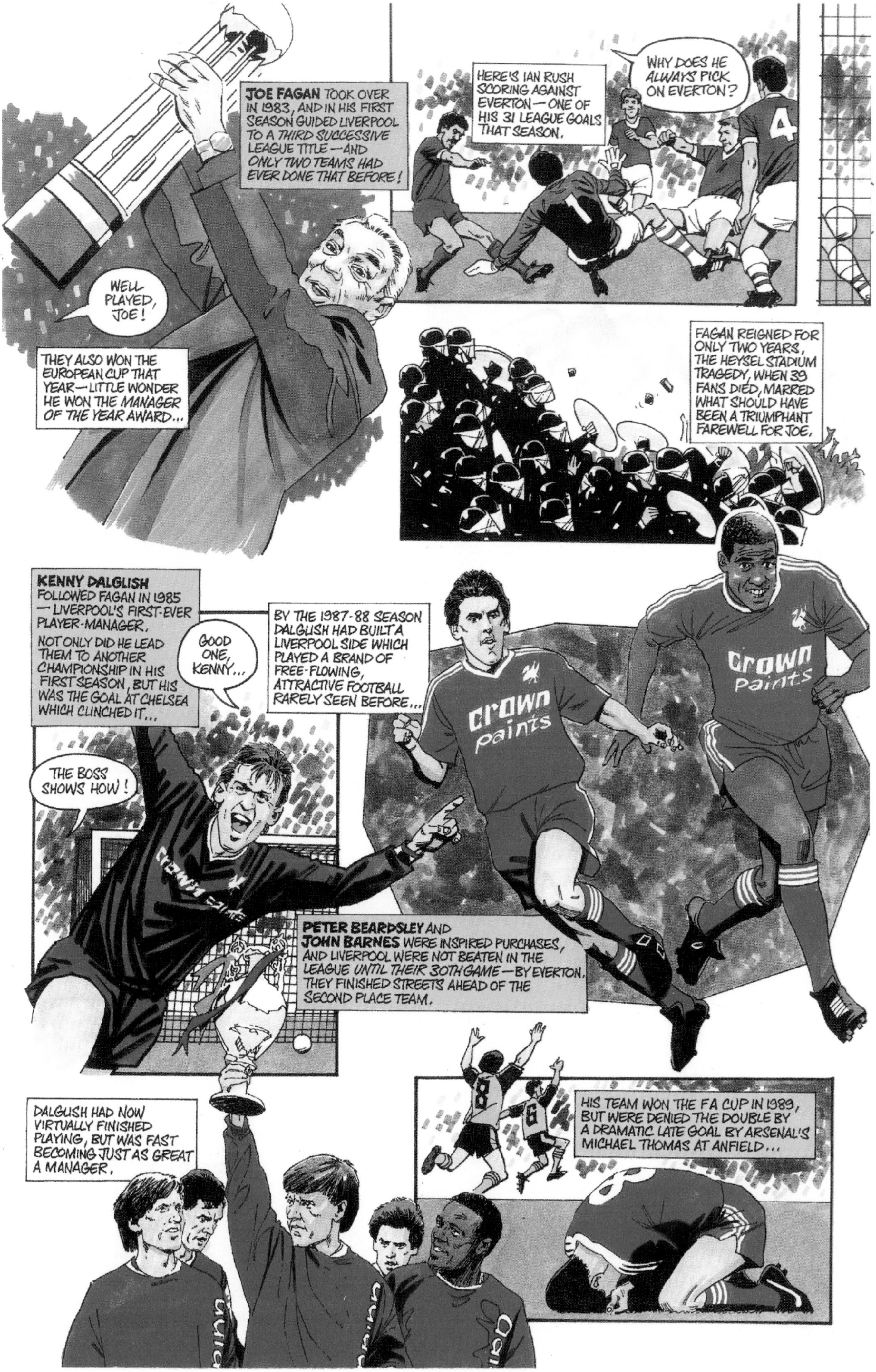
JOE FAGAN TOOK OVER IN 1983, AND IN HIS FIRST SEASON GUIDED LIVERPOOL TO A THIRD SUCCESSIVE LEAGUE TITLE — AND ONLY TWO TEAMS HAD EVER DONE THAT BEFORE!
HERE'S IAN RUSH SCORING AGAINST EVERTON — ONE OF HIS 31 LEAGUE GOALS THAT SEASON.
WHY DOES HE ALWAYS PICK ON EVERTON?
WELL PLAYED, JOE!
THEY ALSO WON THE EUROPEAN CUP THAT YEAR — LITTLE WONDER HE WON THE MANAGER OF THE YEAR AWARD...
FAGAN REIGNED FOR ONLY TWO YEARS, THE HEYSEL STADIUM TRAGEDY, WHEN 39 FANS DIED, MARRED WHAT SHOULD HAVE BEEN A TRIUMPHANT FAREWELL FOR JOE.
KENNY DALGLISH FOLLOWED FAGAN IN 1985 — LIVERPOOL'S FIRST-EVER PLAYER-MANAGER.
NOT ONLY DID HE LEAD THEM TO ANOTHER CHAMPIONSHIP IN HIS FIRST SEASON, BUT HIS WAS THE GOAL AT CHELSEA WHICH CLINCHED IT...
GOOD ONE, KENNY...
BY THE 1987-88 SEASON DALGLISH HAD BUILT A LIVERPOOL SIDE WHICH PLAYED A BRAND OF FREE-FLOWING, ATTRACTIVE FOOTBALL RARELY SEEN BEFORE...
Crown paints
Crown paints
THE BOSS SHOWS HOW!
PETER BEARDSLEY AND JOHN BARNES WERE INSPIRED PURCHASES, AND LIVERPOOL WERE NOT BEATEN IN THE LEAGUE UNTIL THEIR 30TH GAME — BY EVERTON. THEY FINISHED STREETS AHEAD OF THE SECOND PLACE TEAM.
DALGLISH HAD NOW VIRTUALLY FINISHED PLAYING, BUT WAS FAST BECOMING JUST AS GREAT A MANAGER.
HIS TEAM WON THE FA CUP IN 1989, BUT WERE DENIED THE DOUBLE BY A DRAMATIC LATE GOAL BY ARSENAL'S MICHAEL THOMAS AT ANFIELD...

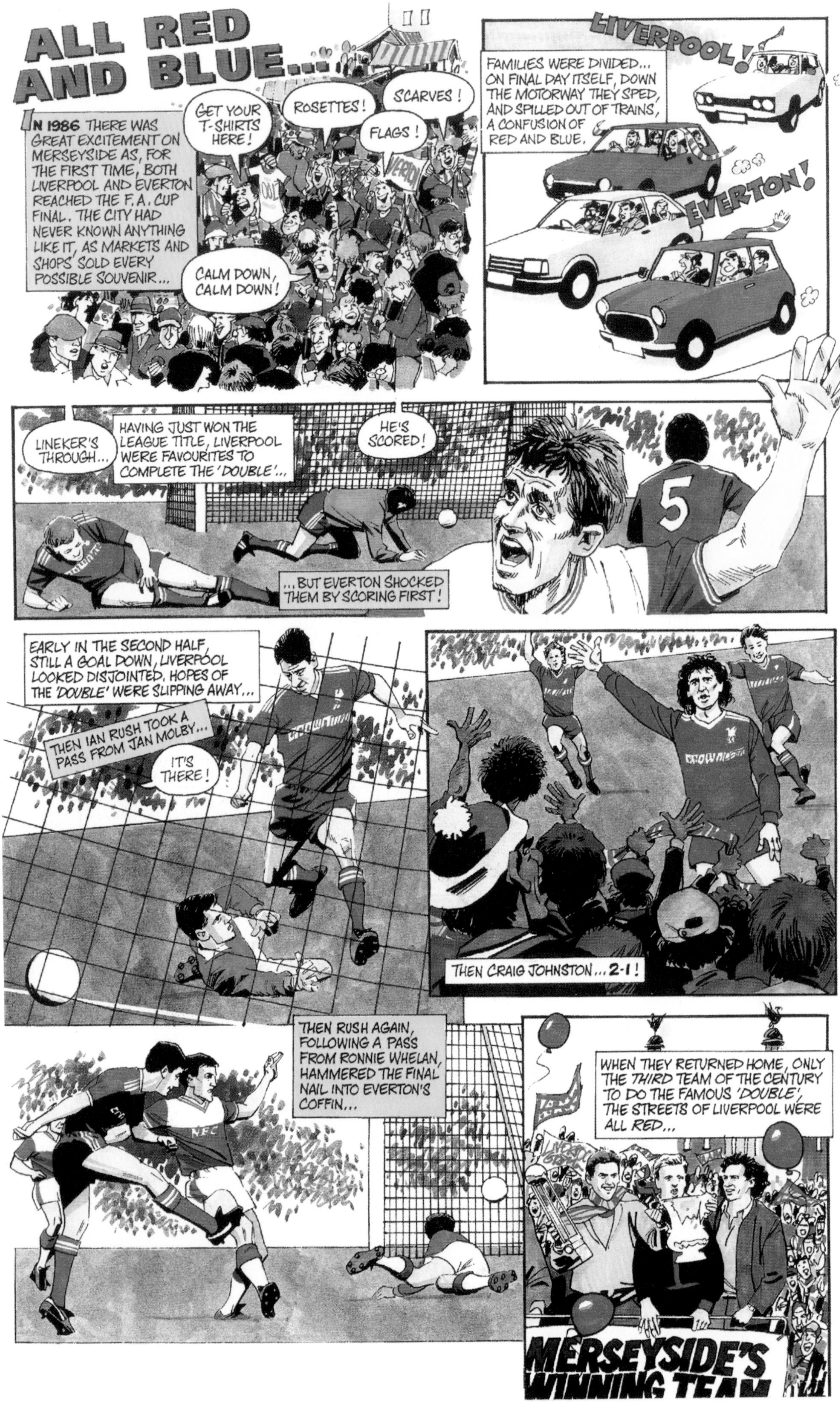
ALL RED AND BLUE...
IN 1986 THERE WAS GREAT EXCITEMENT ON MERSEYSIDE AS, FOR THE FIRST TIME, BOTH LIVERPOOL AND EVERTON REACHED THE F. A. CUP FINAL. THE CITY HAD NEVER KNOWN ANYTHING LIKE IT, AS MARKETS AND SHOPS SOLD EVERY POSSIBLE SOUVENIR...
GET YOUR T-SHIRTS HERE!
ROSETTES!
SCARVES!
FLAGS!
CALM DOWN, CALM DOWN!
FAMILIES WERE DIVIDED... ON FINAL DAY ITSELF, DOWN THE MOTORWAY THEY SPED, AND SPILLED OUT OF TRAINS, A CONFUSION OF RED AND BLUE.
LIVERPOOL!
EVERTON!
LINEKER'S THROUGH...
HAVING JUST WON THE LEAGUE TITLE, LIVERPOOL WERE FAVOURITES TO COMPLETE THE 'DOUBLE'...
HE'S SCORED!
...BUT EVERTON SHOCKED THEM BY SCORING FIRST!
EARLY IN THE SECOND HALF, STILL A GOAL DOWN, LIVERPOOL LOOKED DISJOINTED. HOPES OF THE 'DOUBLE' WERE SLIPPING AWAY...
THEN IAN RUSH TOOK A PASS FROM JAN MOLBY...
IT'S THERE!
THEN CRAIG JOHNSTON... 2-1!
THEN RUSH AGAIN, FOLLOWING A PASS FROM RONNIE WHELAN, HAMMERED THE FINAL NAIL INTO EVERTON'S COFFIN...
WHEN THEY RETURNED HOME, ONLY THE THIRD TEAM OF THE CENTURY TO DO THE FAMOUS 'DOUBLE', THE STREETS OF LIVERPOOL WERE ALL RED...
MERSEYSIDE'S WINNING TEAM

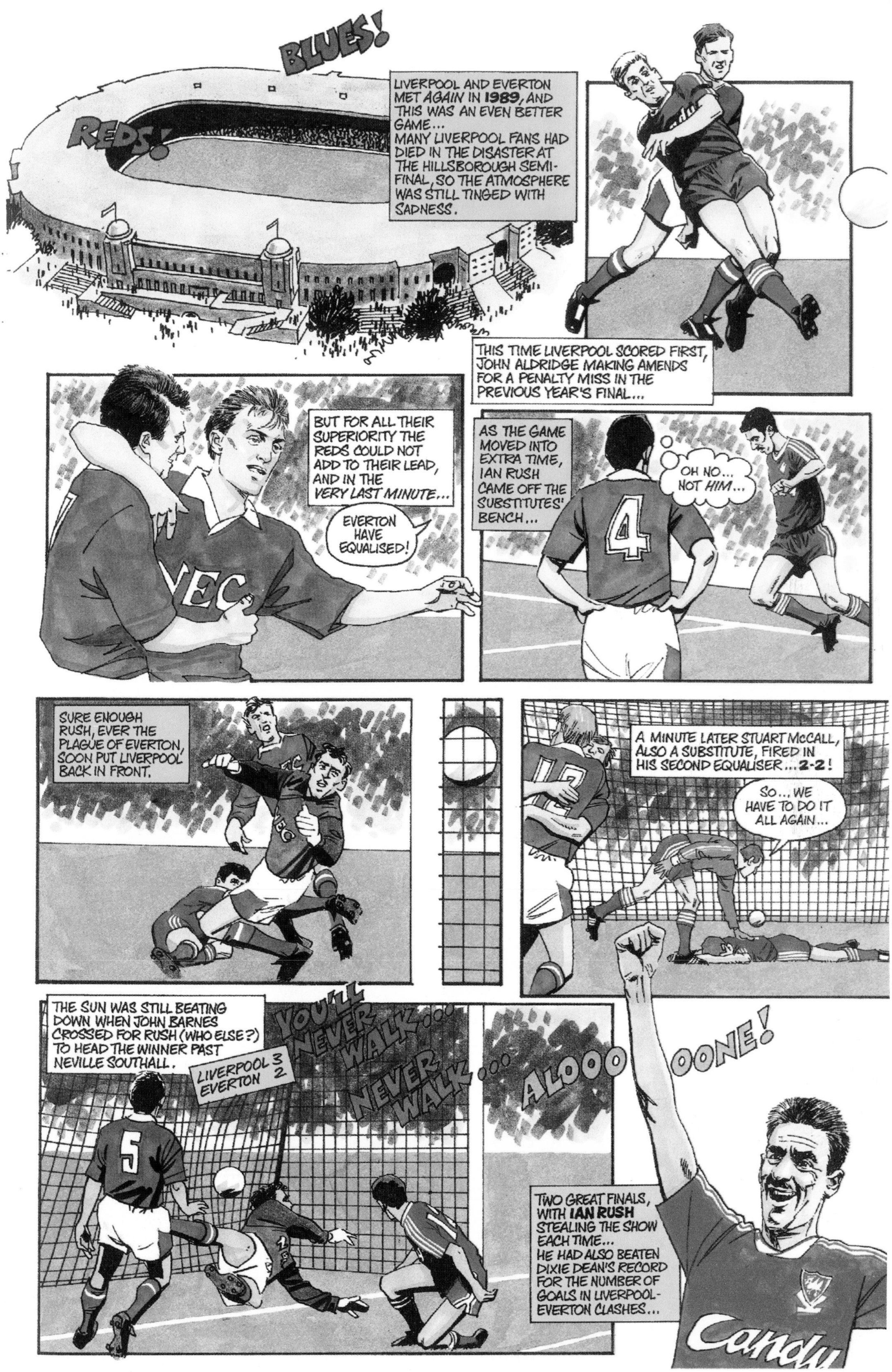
BLUES!
REDS!
LIVERPOOL AND EVERTON MET AGAIN IN 1989, AND THIS WAS AN EVEN BETTER GAME...
MANY LIVERPOOL FANS HAD DIED IN THE DISASTER AT THE HILLSBOROUGH SEMI-FINAL, SO THE ATMOSPHERE WAS STILL TINGED WITH SADNESS.
THIS TIME LIVERPOOL SCORED FIRST, JOHN ALDRIDGE MAKING AMENDS FOR A PENALTY MISS IN THE PREVIOUS YEAR'S FINAL...
BUT FOR ALL THEIR SUPERIORITY THE REDS COULD NOT ADD TO THEIR LEAD, AND IN THE VERY LAST MINUTE...
EVERTON HAVE EQUALISED!
AS THE GAME MOVED INTO EXTRA TIME, IAN RUSH CAME OFF THE SUBSTITUTES' BENCH...
OH NO... NOT HIM...
SURE ENOUGH RUSH, EVER THE PLAGUE OF EVERTON, SOON PUT LIVERPOOL BACK IN FRONT.
A MINUTE LATER STUART McCALL, ALSO A SUBSTITUTE, FIRED IN HIS SECOND EQUALISER... 2-2!
SO... WE HAVE TO DO IT ALL AGAIN...
THE SUN WAS STILL BEATING DOWN WHEN JOHN BARNES CROSSED FOR RUSH (WHO ELSE?) TO HEAD THE WINNER PAST NEVILLE SOUTHALL.
LIVERPOOL 3
EVERTON 2
YOU'LL NEVER WALK...
NEVER WALK...
ALOOO OONE!
TWO GREAT FINALS, WITH IAN RUSH STEALING THE SHOW EACH TIME...
HE HAD ALSO BEATEN DIXIE DEAN'S RECORD FOR THE NUMBER OF GOALS IN LIVERPOOL-EVERTON CLASHES...

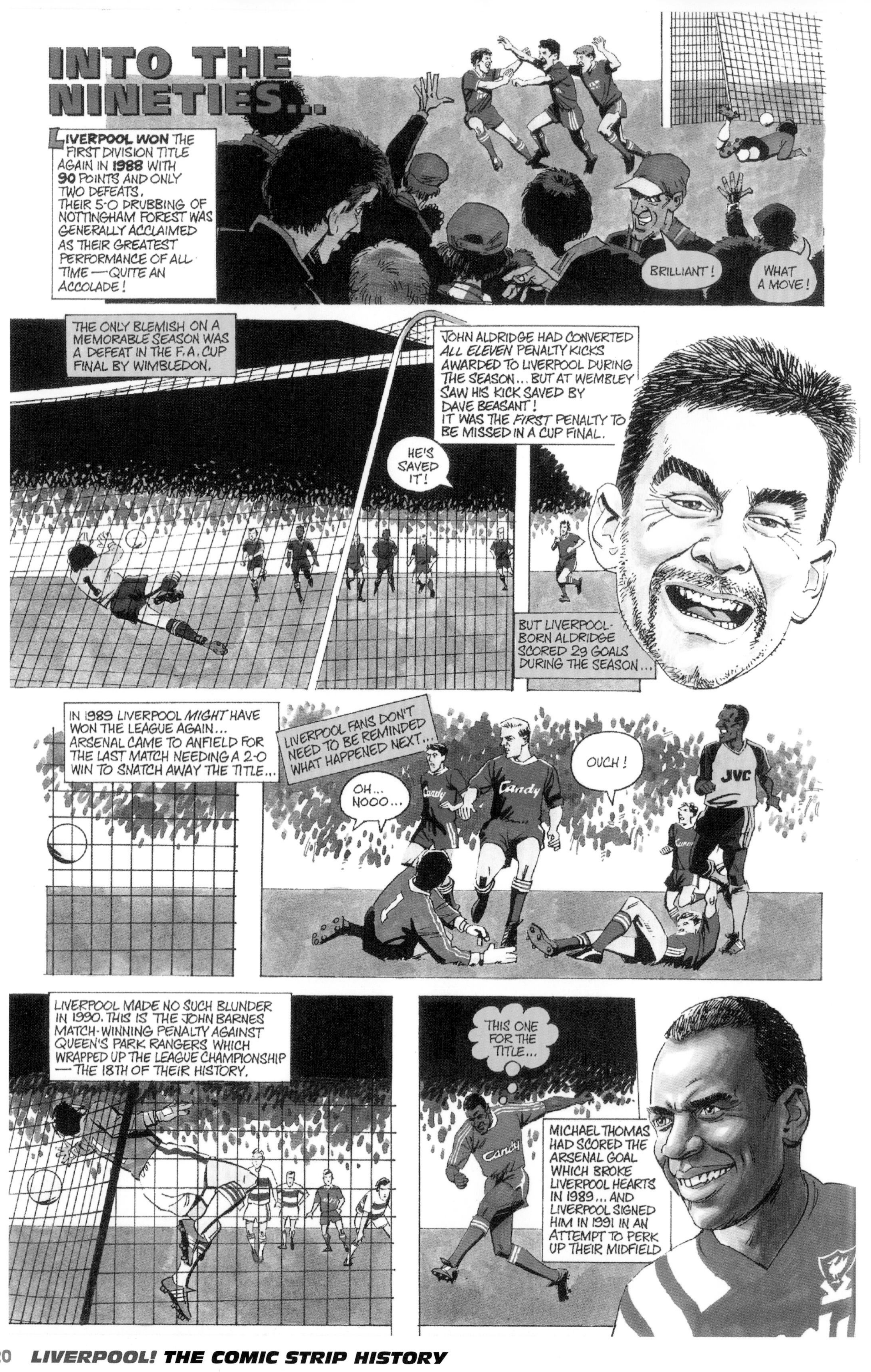
INTO THE NINETIES...
LIVERPOOL WON THE FIRST DIVISION TITLE AGAIN IN 1988 WITH 90 POINTS AND ONLY TWO DEFEATS. THEIR 5-0 DRUBBING OF NOTTINGHAM FOREST WAS GENERALLY ACCLAIMED AS THEIR GREATEST PERFORMANCE OF ALL TIME — QUITE AN ACCOLADE!
BRILLIANT!
WHAT A MOVE!
THE ONLY BLEMISH ON A MEMORABLE SEASON WAS A DEFEAT IN THE F.A. CUP FINAL BY WIMBLEDON.
JOHN ALDRIDGE HAD CONVERTED ALL ELEVEN PENALTY KICKS AWARDED TO LIVERPOOL DURING THE SEASON... BUT AT WEMBLEY SAW HIS KICK SAVED BY DAVE BEASANT! IT WAS THE FIRST PENALTY TO BE MISSED IN A CUP FINAL.
HE'S SAVED IT!
BUT LIVERPOOL-BORN ALDRIDGE SCORED 29 GOALS DURING THE SEASON...
IN 1989 LIVERPOOL MIGHT HAVE WON THE LEAGUE AGAIN... ARSENAL CAME TO ANFIELD FOR THE LAST MATCH NEEDING A 2-0 WIN TO SNATCH AWAY THE TITLE...
LIVERPOOL FANS DON'T NEED TO BE REMINDED WHAT HAPPENED NEXT...
OH... NOOO...
OUCH!
LIVERPOOL MADE NO SUCH BLUNDER IN 1990. THIS IS THE JOHN BARNES MATCH-WINNING PENALTY AGAINST QUEEN'S PARK RANGERS WHICH WRAPPED UP THE LEAGUE CHAMPIONSHIP — THE 18TH OF THEIR HISTORY.
THIS ONE FOR THE TITLE...
MICHAEL THOMAS HAD SCORED THE ARSENAL GOAL WHICH BROKE LIVERPOOL HEARTS IN 1989... AND LIVERPOOL SIGNED HIM IN 1991 IN AN ATTEMPT TO PERK UP THEIR MIDFIELD

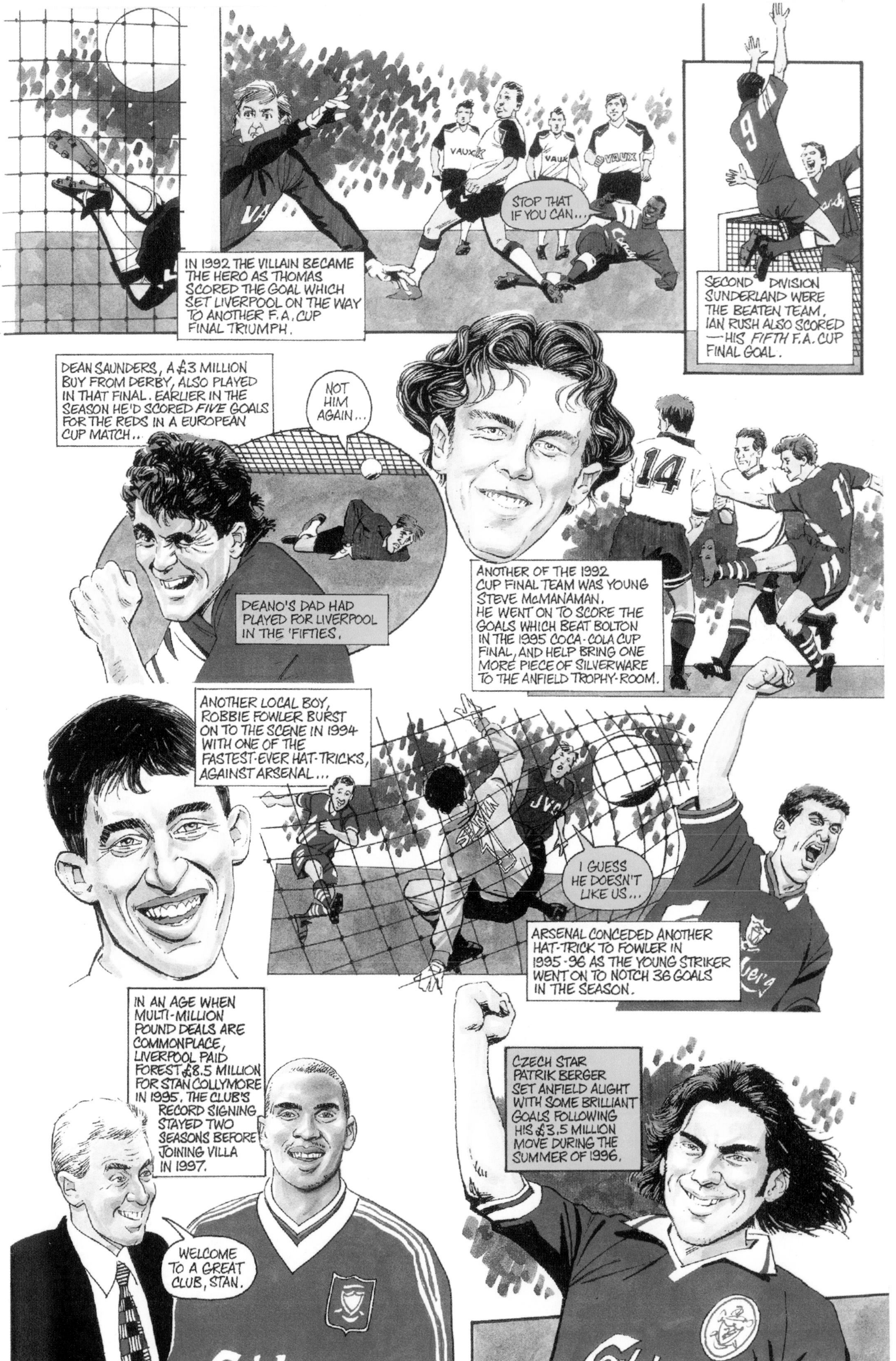
IN 1992 THE VILLAIN BECAME THE HERO AS THOMAS SCORED THE GOAL WHICH SET LIVERPOOL ON THE WAY TO ANOTHER F.A. CUP FINAL TRIUMPH.
STOP THAT IF YOU CAN...
SECOND DIVISION SUNDERLAND WERE THE BEATEN TEAM. IAN RUSH ALSO SCORED — HIS *FIFTH* F.A. CUP FINAL GOAL.
DEAN SAUNDERS, A £3 MILLION BUY FROM DERBY, ALSO PLAYED IN THAT FINAL. EARLIER IN THE SEASON HE'D SCORED *FIVE* GOALS FOR THE REDS IN A EUROPEAN CUP MATCH...
NOT HIM AGAIN...
DEANO'S DAD HAD PLAYED FOR LIVERPOOL IN THE 'FIFTIES.
ANOTHER OF THE 1992 CUP FINAL TEAM WAS YOUNG STEVE McMANAMAN. HE WENT ON TO SCORE THE GOALS WHICH BEAT BOLTON IN THE 1995 COCA-COLA CUP FINAL, AND HELP BRING ONE MORE PIECE OF SILVERWARE TO THE ANFIELD TROPHY-ROOM.
ANOTHER LOCAL BOY, ROBBIE FOWLER BURST ON TO THE SCENE IN 1994 WITH ONE OF THE FASTEST-EVER HAT-TRICKS, AGAINST ARSENAL...
I GUESS HE DOESN'T LIKE US...
ARSENAL CONCEDED ANOTHER HAT-TRICK TO FOWLER IN 1995-96 AS THE YOUNG STRIKER WENT ON TO NOTCH 36 GOALS IN THE SEASON.
IN AN AGE WHEN MULTI-MILLION POUND DEALS ARE COMMONPLACE, LIVERPOOL PAID FOREST £8.5 MILLION FOR STAN COLLYMORE IN 1995. THE CLUB'S RECORD SIGNING STAYED TWO SEASONS BEFORE JOINING VILLA IN 1997.
WELCOME TO A GREAT CLUB, STAN.
CZECH STAR PATRIK BERGER SET ANFIELD ALIGHT WITH SOME BRILLIANT GOALS FOLLOWING HIS £3.5 MILLION MOVE DURING THE SUMMER OF 1996.

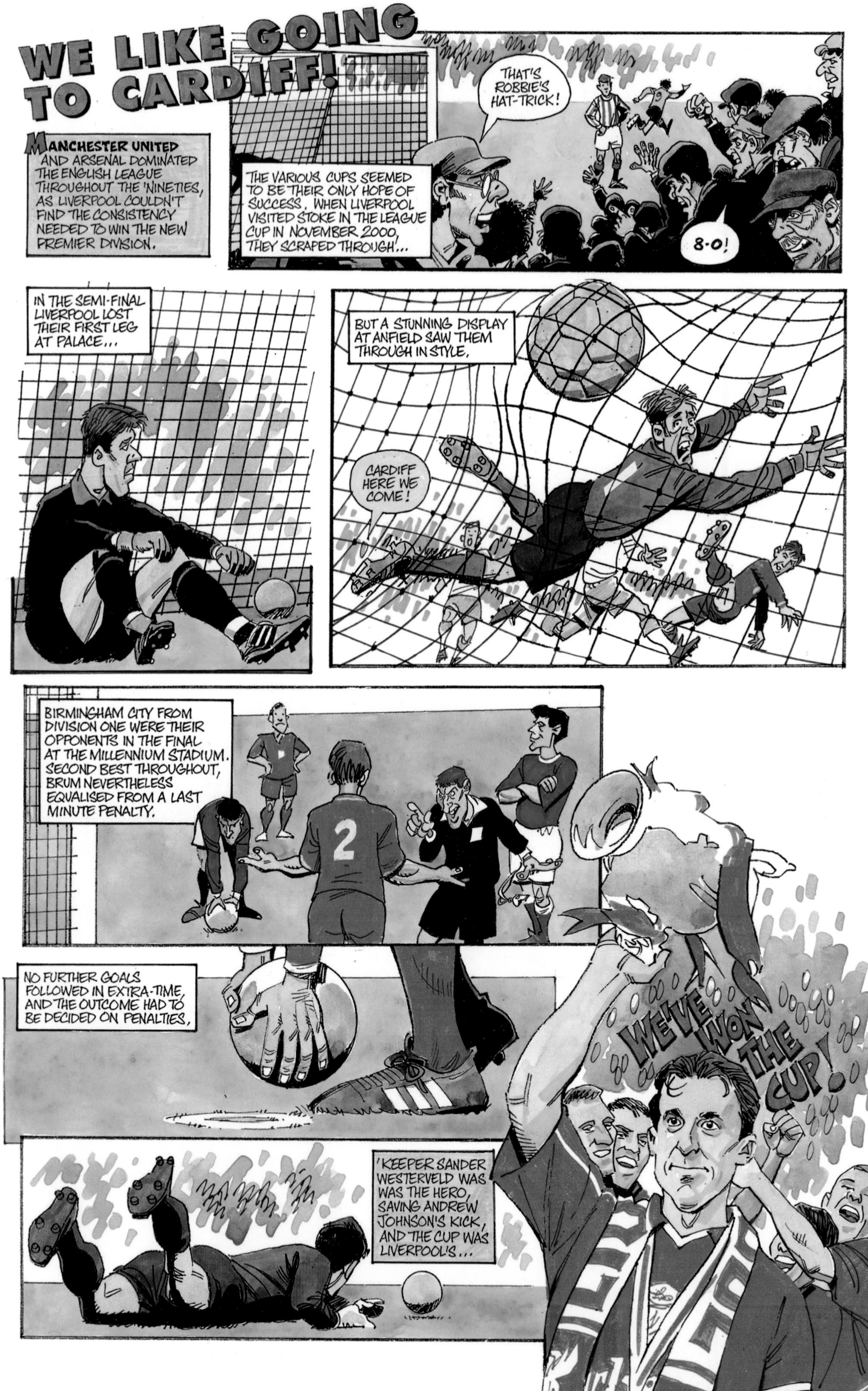
WE LIKE GOING TO CARDIFF!
MANCHESTER UNITED AND ARSENAL DOMINATED THE ENGLISH LEAGUE THROUGHOUT THE 'NINETIES, AS LIVERPOOL COULDN'T FIND THE CONSISTENCY NEEDED TO WIN THE NEW PREMIER DIVISION.
THE VARIOUS CUPS SEEMED TO BE THEIR ONLY HOPE OF SUCCESS. WHEN LIVERPOOL VISITED STOKE IN THE LEAGUE CUP IN NOVEMBER 2000, THEY SCRAPED THROUGH!...
THAT'S ROBBIE'S HAT-TRICK!
8-0!
IN THE SEMI-FINAL LIVERPOOL LOST THEIR FIRST LEG AT PALACE...
BUT A STUNNING DISPLAY AT ANFIELD SAW THEM THROUGH IN STYLE.
CARDIFF HERE WE COME!
BIRMINGHAM CITY FROM DIVISION ONE WERE THEIR OPPONENTS IN THE FINAL AT THE MILLENNIUM STADIUM. SECOND BEST THROUGHOUT, BRUM NEVERTHELESS EQUALISED FROM A LAST MINUTE PENALTY.
NO FURTHER GOALS FOLLOWED IN EXTRA-TIME, AND THE OUTCOME HAD TO BE DECIDED ON PENALTIES.
'KEEPER SANDER WESTERVELD WAS THE HERO, SAVING ANDREW JOHNSON'S KICK, AND THE CUP WAS LIVERPOOL'S...
WE'VE WON THE CUP!

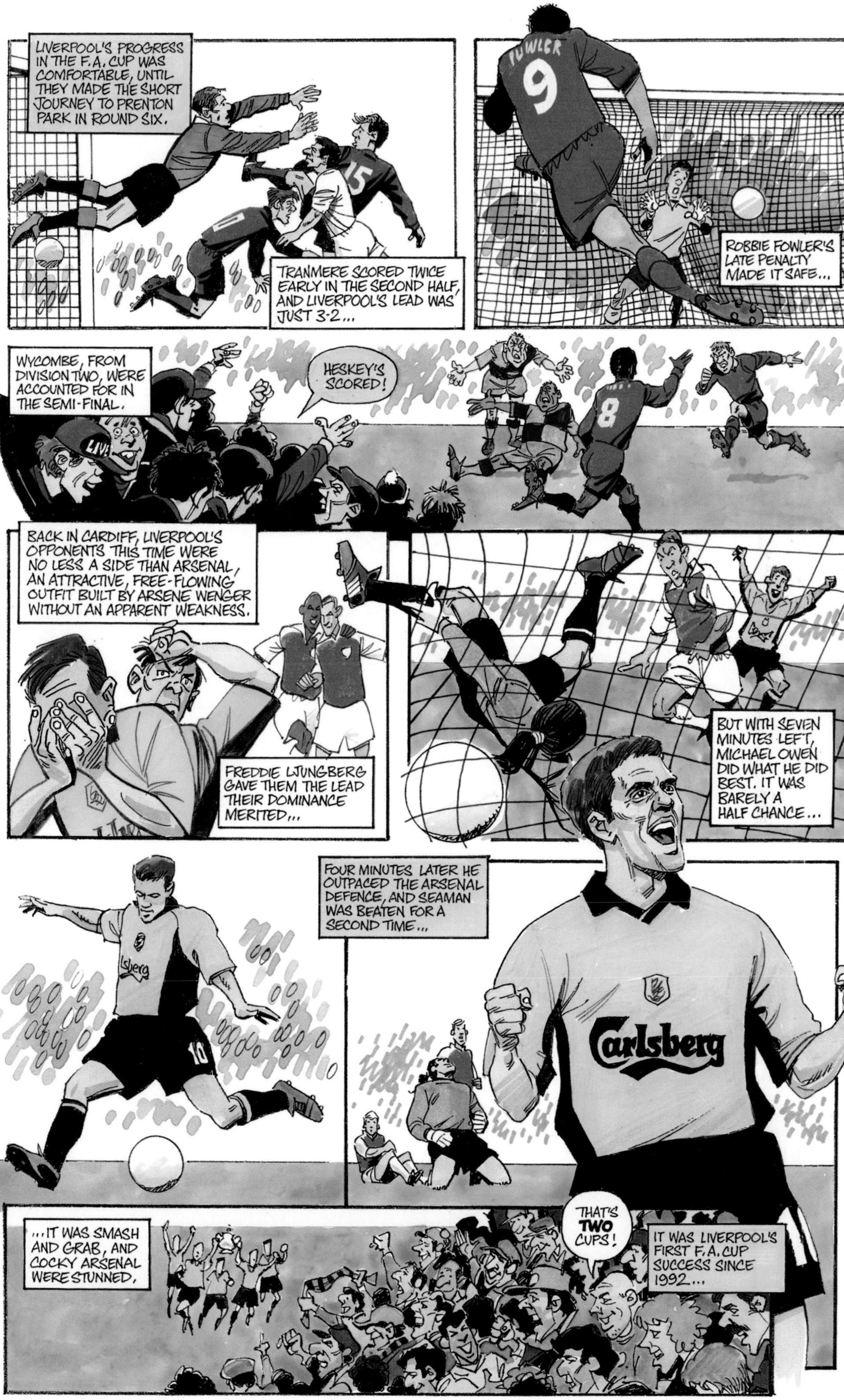
LIVERPOOL'S PROGRESS IN THE F.A. CUP WAS COMFORTABLE, UNTIL THEY MADE THE SHORT JOURNEY TO PRENTON PARK IN ROUND SIX.
TRANMERE SCORED TWICE EARLY IN THE SECOND HALF, AND LIVERPOOL'S LEAD WAS JUST 3-2...
FOWLER
9
ROBBIE FOWLER'S LATE PENALTY MADE IT SAFE...
WYCOMBE, FROM DIVISION TWO, WERE ACCOUNTED FOR IN THE SEMI-FINAL.
HESKEY'S SCORED!
BACK IN CARDIFF, LIVERPOOL'S OPPONENTS THIS TIME WERE NO LESS A SIDE THAN ARSENAL, AN ATTRACTIVE, FREE-FLOWING OUTFIT BUILT BY ARSENE WENGER WITHOUT AN APPARENT WEAKNESS.
FREDDIE LJUNGBERG GAVE THEM THE LEAD THEIR DOMINANCE MERITED...
BUT WITH SEVEN MINUTES LEFT, MICHAEL OWEN DID WHAT HE DID BEST. IT WAS BARELY A HALF CHANCE...
FOUR MINUTES LATER HE OUTPACED THE ARSENAL DEFENCE, AND SEAMAN WAS BEATEN FOR A SECOND TIME...
Carlsberg
...IT WAS SMASH AND GRAB, AND COCKY ARSENAL WERE STUNNED.
THAT'S **TWO** CUPS!
IT WAS LIVERPOOL'S FIRST F.A. CUP SUCCESS SINCE 1992...

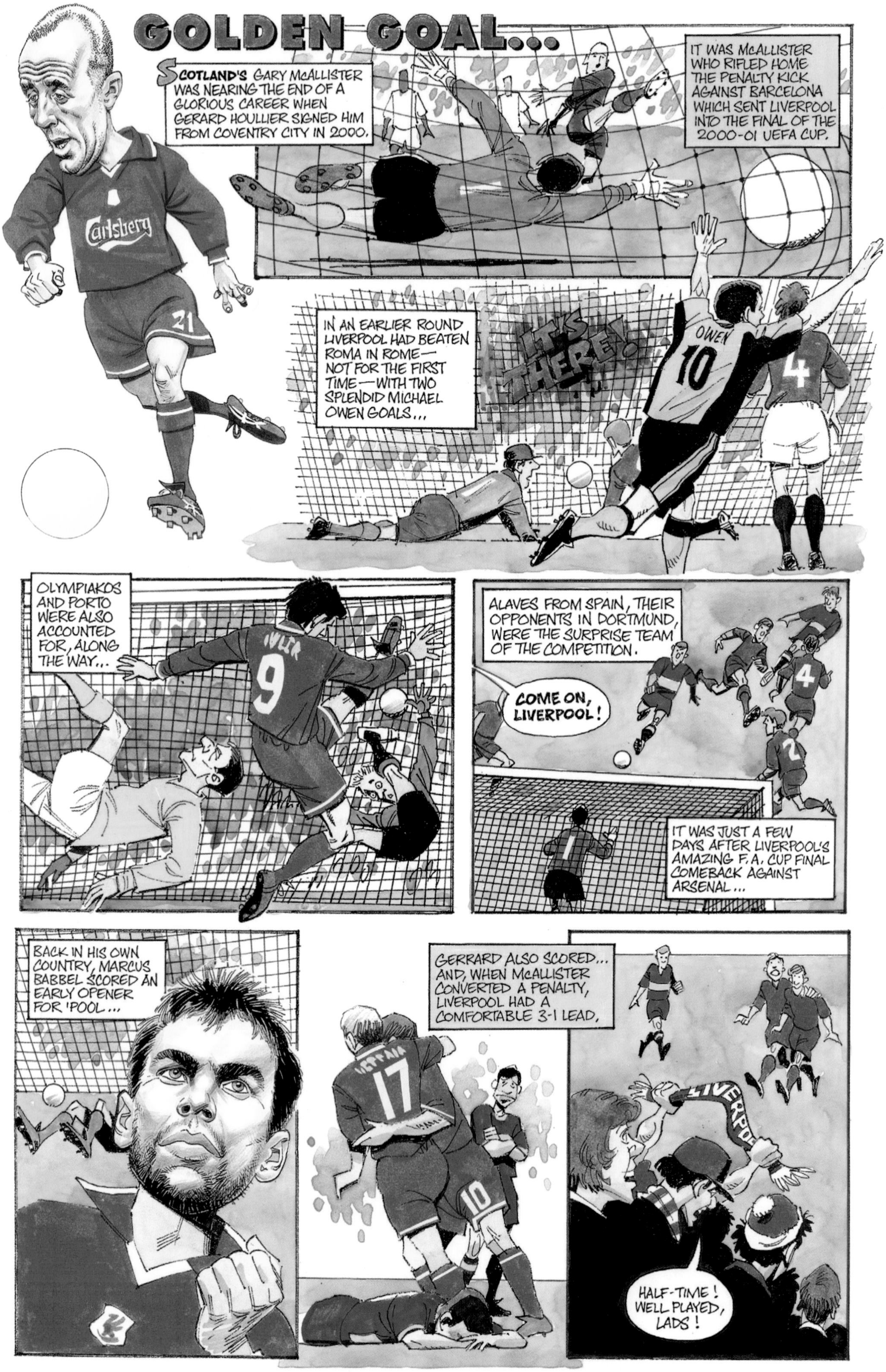
GOLDEN GOAL...
SCOTLAND'S GARY McALLISTER WAS NEARING THE END OF A GLORIOUS CAREER WHEN GERARD HOULLIER SIGNED HIM FROM COVENTRY CITY IN 2000.
IT WAS McALLISTER WHO RIFLED HOME THE PENALTY KICK AGAINST BARCELONA WHICH SENT LIVERPOOL INTO THE FINAL OF THE 2000-01 UEFA CUP.
IN AN EARLIER ROUND LIVERPOOL HAD BEATEN ROMA IN ROME— NOT FOR THE FIRST TIME—WITH TWO SPLENDID MICHAEL OWEN GOALS...
IT'S THERE!
OWEN
OLYMPIAKOS AND PORTO WERE ALSO ACCOUNTED FOR, ALONG THE WAY...
ALAVES FROM SPAIN, THEIR OPPONENTS IN DORTMUND, WERE THE SURPRISE TEAM OF THE COMPETITION.
COME ON, LIVERPOOL!
IT WAS JUST A FEW DAYS AFTER LIVERPOOL'S AMAZING F.A. CUP FINAL COMEBACK AGAINST ARSENAL...
BACK IN HIS OWN COUNTRY, MARCUS BABBEL SCORED AN EARLY OPENER FOR 'POOL...
GERRARD ALSO SCORED... AND, WHEN McALLISTER CONVERTED A PENALTY, LIVERPOOL HAD A COMFORTABLE 3-1 LEAD.
LIVERPOOL
HALF-TIME! WELL PLAYED, LADS!

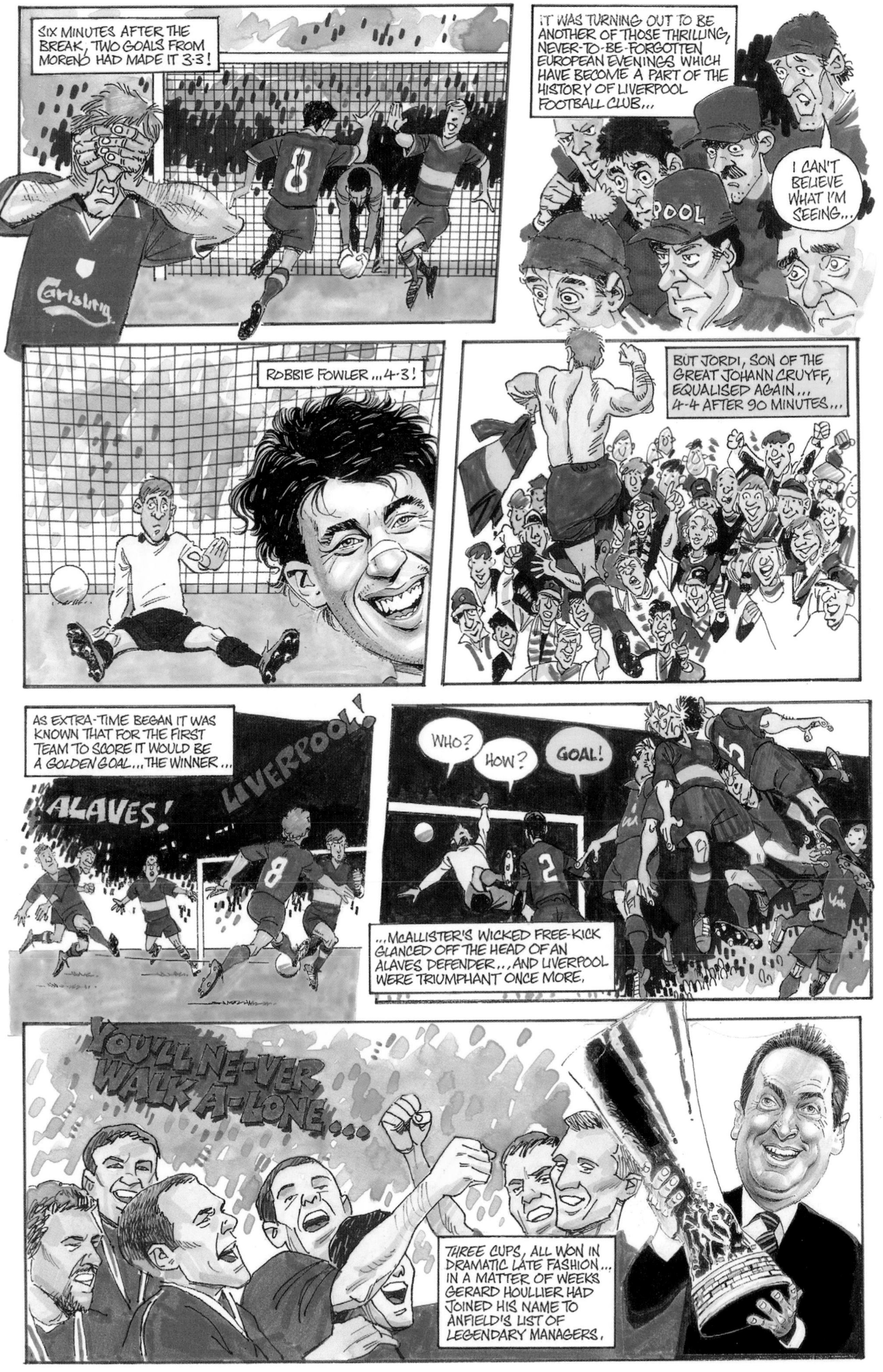
SIX MINUTES AFTER THE BREAK, TWO GOALS FROM MORENO HAD MADE IT 3-3!
IT WAS TURNING OUT TO BE ANOTHER OF THOSE THRILLING, NEVER-TO-BE-FORGOTTEN EUROPEAN EVENINGS WHICH HAVE BECOME A PART OF THE HISTORY OF LIVERPOOL FOOTBALL CLUB...
POOL
I CAN'T BELIEVE WHAT I'M SEEING...
ROBBIE FOWLER...4-3!
BUT JORDI, SON OF THE GREAT JOHANN CRUYFF, EQUALISED AGAIN... 4-4 AFTER 90 MINUTES...
AS EXTRA-TIME BEGAN IT WAS KNOWN THAT FOR THE FIRST TEAM TO SCORE IT WOULD BE A GOLDEN GOAL...THE WINNER...
LIVERPOOL!
ALAVES!
WHO?
HOW?
GOAL!
...McALLISTER'S WICKED FREE-KICK GLANCED OFF THE HEAD OF AN ALAVES DEFENDER..., AND LIVERPOOL WERE TRIUMPHANT ONCE MORE.
YOU'LL NE-VER WALK A-LONE...
THREE CUPS, ALL WON IN DRAMATIC LATE FASHION... IN A MATTER OF WEEKS GERARD HOULLIER HAD JOINED HIS NAME TO ANFIELD'S LIST OF LEGENDARY MANAGERS.

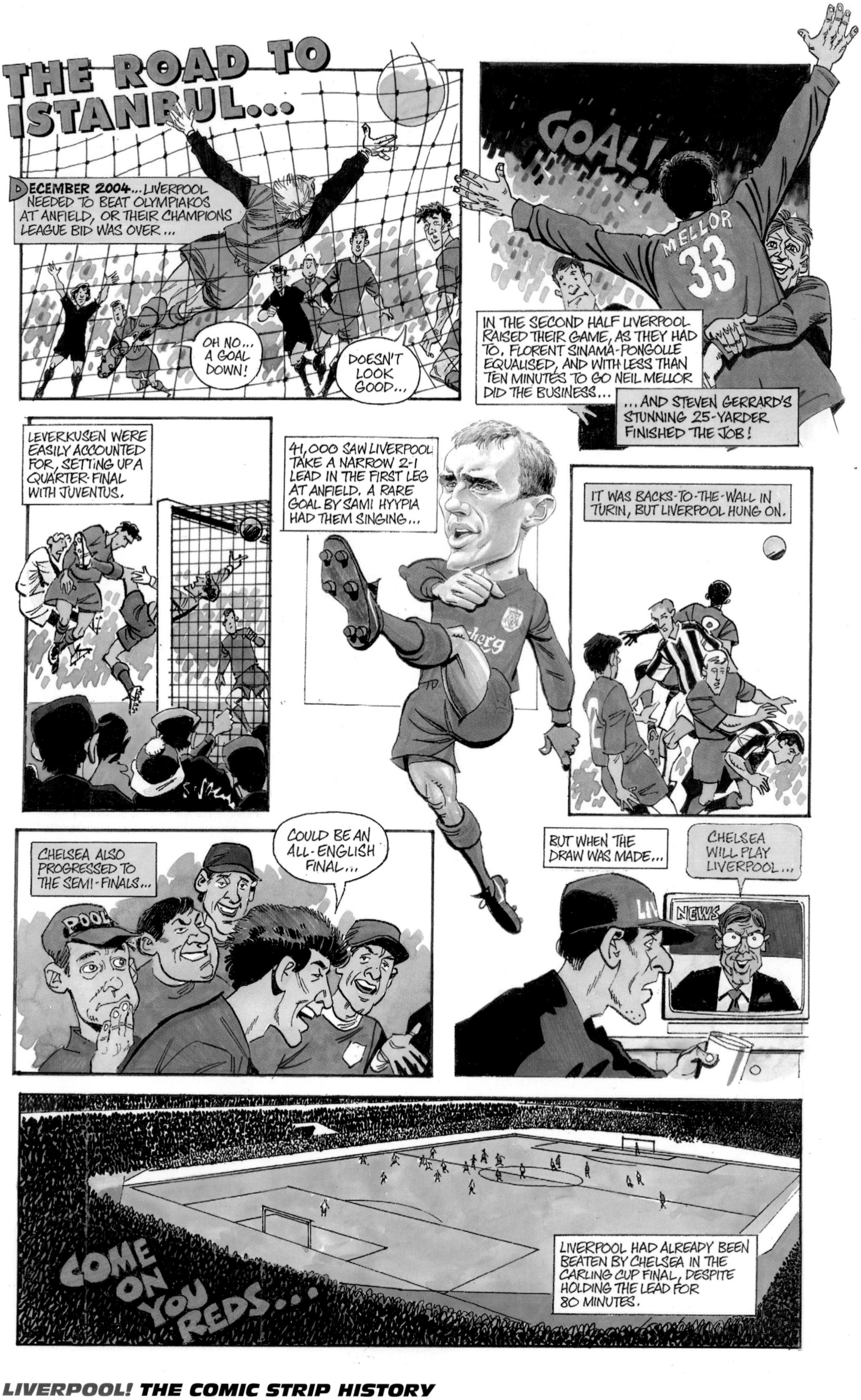
THE ROAD TO ISTANBUL...
DECEMBER 2004... LIVERPOOL NEEDED TO BEAT OLYMPIAKOS AT ANFIELD, OR THEIR CHAMPIONS LEAGUE BID WAS OVER...
OH NO... A GOAL DOWN!
DOESN'T LOOK GOOD...
GOAL!
MELLOR 33
IN THE SECOND HALF LIVERPOOL RAISED THEIR GAME, AS THEY HAD TO. FLORENT SINAMA-PONGOLLE EQUALISED, AND WITH LESS THAN TEN MINUTES TO GO NEIL MELLOR DID THE BUSINESS...
...AND STEVEN GERRARD'S STUNNING 25-YARDER FINISHED THE JOB!
LEVERKUSEN WERE EASILY ACCOUNTED FOR, SETTING UP A QUARTER-FINAL WITH JUVENTUS.
41,000 SAW LIVERPOOL TAKE A NARROW 2-1 LEAD IN THE FIRST LEG AT ANFIELD. A RARE GOAL BY SAMI HYYPIA HAD THEM SINGING...
IT WAS BACKS-TO-THE-WALL IN TURIN, BUT LIVERPOOL HUNG ON.
CHELSEA ALSO PROGRESSED TO THE SEMI-FINALS...
COULD BE AN ALL-ENGLISH FINAL...
POOL
BUT WHEN THE DRAW WAS MADE...
CHELSEA WILL PLAY LIVERPOOL...
NEWS
COME ON YOU REDS...
LIVERPOOL HAD ALREADY BEEN BEATEN BY CHELSEA IN THE CARLING CUP FINAL, DESPITE HOLDING THE LEAD FOR 80 MINUTES.

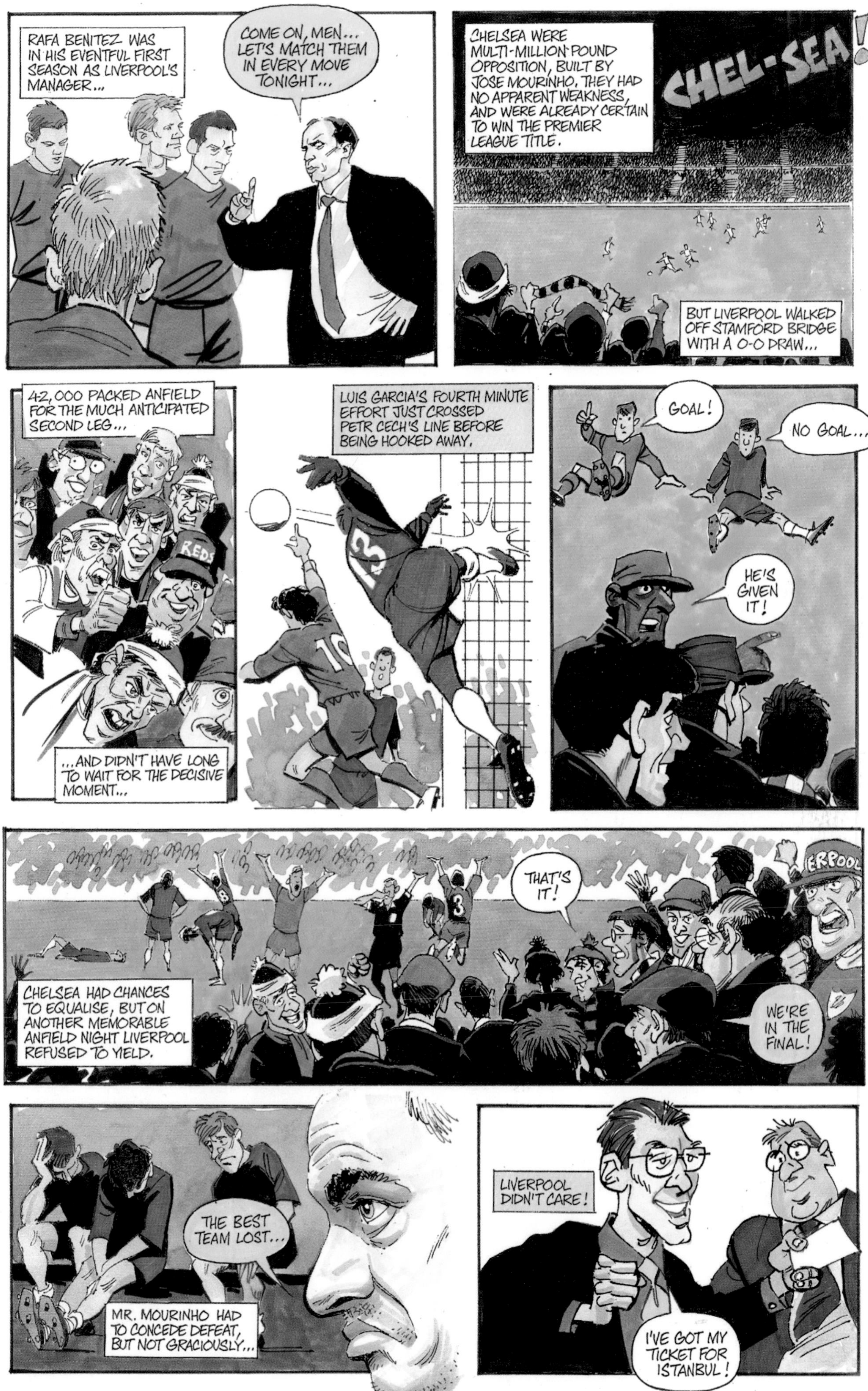

RAFA BENITEZ WAS IN HIS EVENTFUL FIRST SEASON AS LIVERPOOL'S MANAGER...
COME ON, MEN... LET'S MATCH THEM IN EVERY MOVE TONIGHT...
CHELSEA WERE MULTI-MILLION-POUND OPPOSITION, BUILT BY JOSE MOURINHO. THEY HAD NO APPARENT WEAKNESS, AND WERE ALREADY CERTAIN TO WIN THE PREMIER LEAGUE TITLE.
CHEL-SEA!
BUT LIVERPOOL WALKED OFF STAMFORD BRIDGE WITH A 0-0 DRAW...
42,000 PACKED ANFIELD FOR THE MUCH ANTICIPATED SECOND LEG...
REDS
...AND DIDN'T HAVE LONG TO WAIT FOR THE DECISIVE MOMENT...
LUIS GARCIA'S FOURTH MINUTE EFFORT JUST CROSSED PETR CECH'S LINE BEFORE BEING HOOKED AWAY.
GOAL!
NO GOAL...
HE'S GIVEN IT!
THAT'S IT!
ERPOOL
CHELSEA HAD CHANCES TO EQUALISE, BUT ON ANOTHER MEMORABLE ANFIELD NIGHT LIVERPOOL REFUSED TO YIELD.
WE'RE IN THE FINAL!
THE BEST TEAM LOST...
MR. MOURINHO HAD TO CONCEDE DEFEAT, BUT NOT GRACIOUSLY...
LIVERPOOL DIDN'T CARE!
I'VE GOT MY TICKET FOR ISTANBUL!

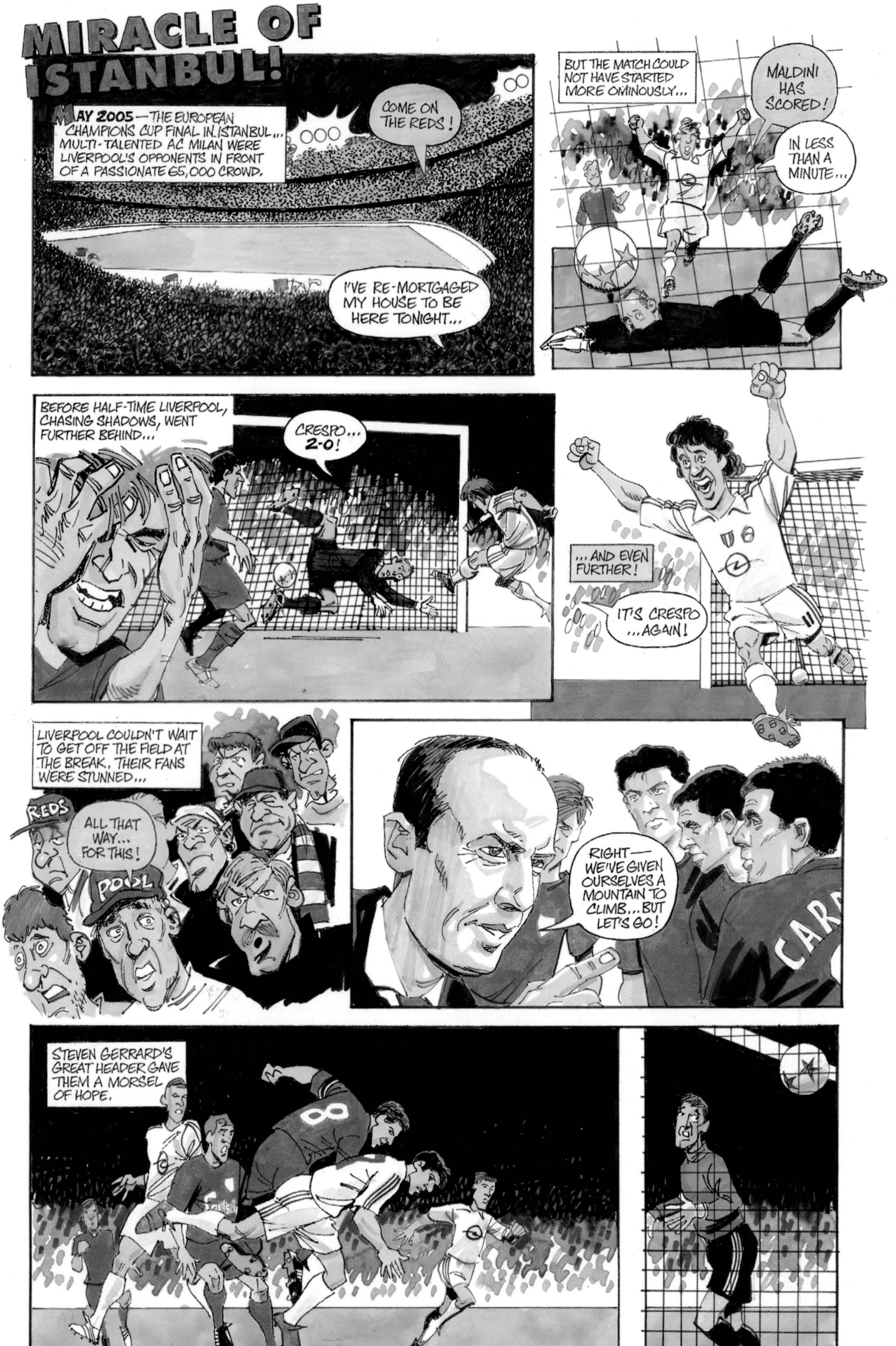
MIRACLE OF ISTANBUL!
MAY 2005—THE EUROPEAN CHAMPIONS CUP FINAL IN ISTANBUL... MULTI-TALENTED AC MILAN WERE LIVERPOOL'S OPPONENTS IN FRONT OF A PASSIONATE 65,000 CROWD.
COME ON THE REDS!
I'VE RE-MORTGAGED MY HOUSE TO BE HERE TONIGHT...
BUT THE MATCH COULD NOT HAVE STARTED MORE OMINOUSLY...
MALDINI HAS SCORED!
IN LESS THAN A MINUTE...
BEFORE HALF-TIME LIVERPOOL, CHASING SHADOWS, WENT FURTHER BEHIND...
CRESPO... 2-0!
...AND EVEN FURTHER!
IT'S CRESPO ...AGAIN!
LIVERPOOL COULDN'T WAIT TO GET OFF THE FIELD AT THE BREAK, THEIR FANS WERE STUNNED...
REDS
ALL THAT WAY... FOR THIS!
POOL
RIGHT— WE'VE GIVEN OURSELVES A MOUNTAIN TO CLIMB... BUT LET'S GO!
STEVEN GERRARD'S GREAT HEADER GAVE THEM A MORSEL OF HOPE.

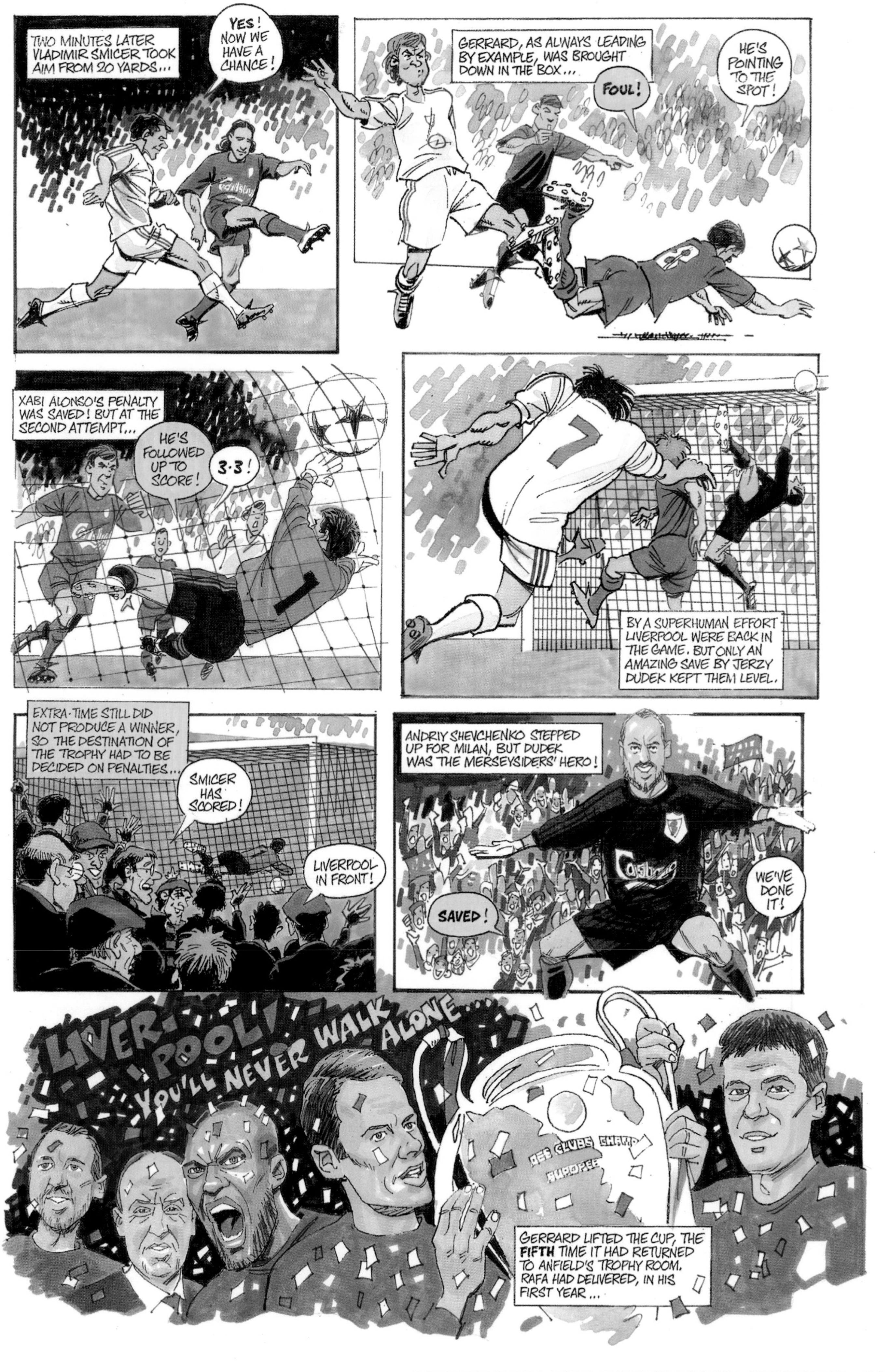
TWO MINUTES LATER VLADIMIR SMICER TOOK AIM FROM 20 YARDS...
YES! NOW WE HAVE A CHANCE!
GERRARD, AS ALWAYS LEADING BY EXAMPLE, WAS BROUGHT DOWN IN THE BOX...
FOUL!
HE'S POINTING TO THE SPOT!
XABI ALONSO'S PENALTY WAS SAVED! BUT AT THE SECOND ATTEMPT...
HE'S FOLLOWED UP TO SCORE!
3-3!
BY A SUPERHUMAN EFFORT LIVERPOOL WERE BACK IN THE GAME. BUT ONLY AN AMAZING SAVE BY JERZY DUDEK KEPT THEM LEVEL.
EXTRA-TIME STILL DID NOT PRODUCE A WINNER, SO THE DESTINATION OF THE TROPHY HAD TO BE DECIDED ON PENALTIES...
SMICER HAS SCORED!
LIVERPOOL IN FRONT!
ANDRIY SHEVCHENKO STEPPED UP FOR MILAN, BUT DUDEK WAS THE MERSEYSIDERS' HERO!
SAVED!
WE'VE DONE IT!
LIVER-POOL! YOU'LL NEVER WALK ALONE...
GERRARD LIFTED THE CUP, THE FIFTH TIME IT HAD RETURNED TO ANFIELD'S TROPHY ROOM. RAFA HAD DELIVERED, IN HIS FIRST YEAR...

MORE MANAGERS...

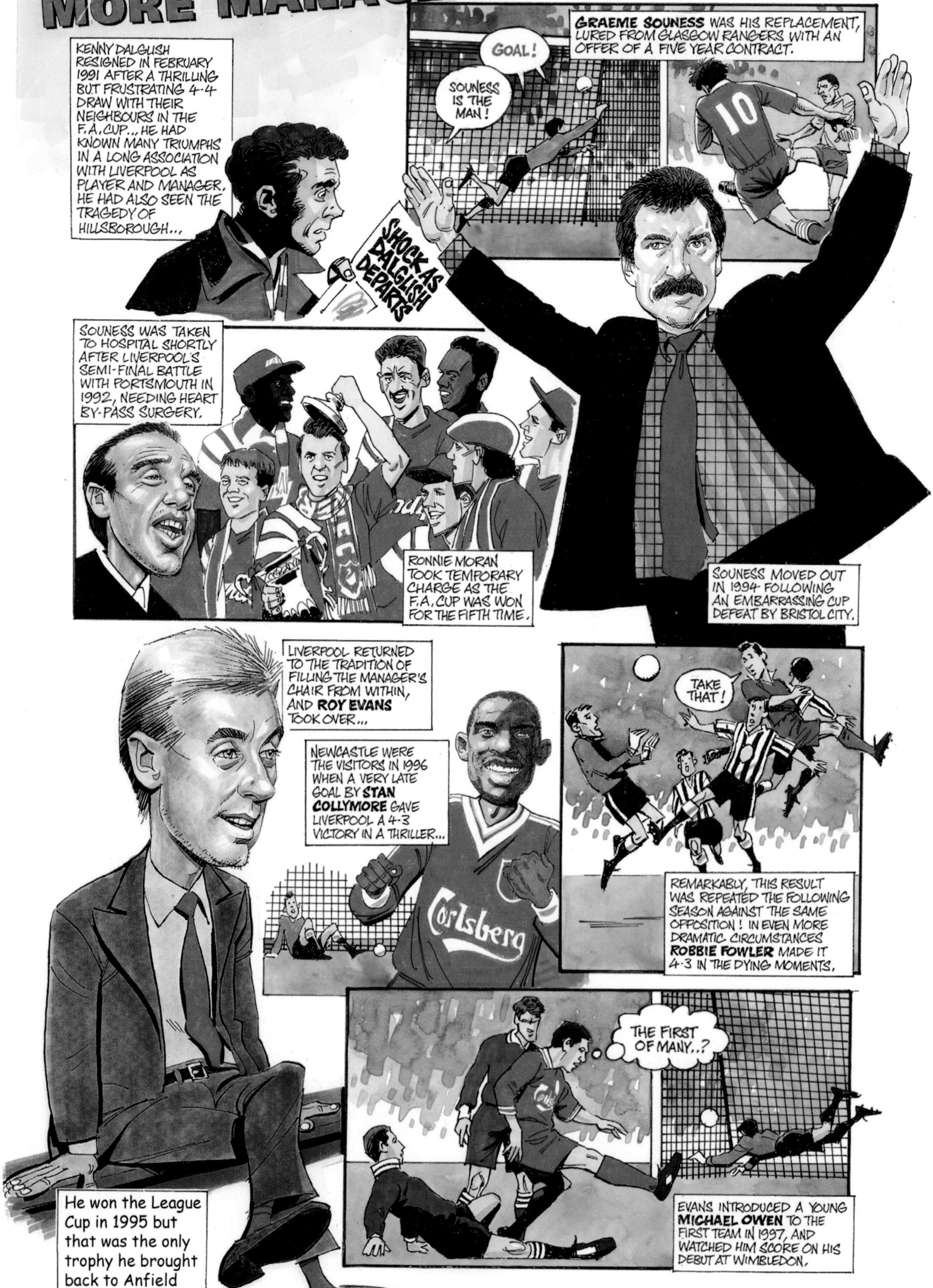
KENNY DALGLISH RESIGNED IN FEBRUARY 1991 AFTER A THRILLING BUT FRUSTRATING 4-4 DRAW WITH THEIR NEIGHBOURS IN THE F.A. CUP... HE HAD KNOWN MANY TRIUMPHS IN A LONG ASSOCIATION WITH LIVERPOOL AS PLAYER AND MANAGER. HE HAD ALSO SEEN THE TRAGEDY OF HILLSBOROUGH...
SHOCK AS DALGLISH DEPARTS
GRAEME SOUNESS WAS HIS REPLACEMENT, LURED FROM GLASGOW RANGERS WITH AN OFFER OF A FIVE YEAR CONTRACT.
GOAL!
SOUNESS IS THE MAN!
SOUNESS WAS TAKEN TO HOSPITAL SHORTLY AFTER LIVERPOOL'S SEMI-FINAL BATTLE WITH PORTSMOUTH IN 1992, NEEDING HEART BY-PASS SURGERY.
RONNIE MORAN TOOK TEMPORARY CHARGE AS THE F.A. CUP WAS WON FOR THE FIFTH TIME.
SOUNESS MOVED OUT IN 1994 FOLLOWING AN EMBARRASSING CUP DEFEAT BY BRISTOL CITY.
LIVERPOOL RETURNED TO THE TRADITION OF FILLING THE MANAGER'S CHAIR FROM WITHIN, AND ROY EVANS TOOK OVER...
NEWCASTLE WERE THE VISITORS IN 1996 WHEN A VERY LATE GOAL BY STAN COLLYMORE GAVE LIVERPOOL A 4-3 VICTORY IN A THRILLER...
Carlsberg
TAKE THAT!
REMARKABLY, THIS RESULT WAS REPEATED THE FOLLOWING SEASON AGAINST THE SAME OPPOSITION! IN EVEN MORE DRAMATIC CIRCUMSTANCES ROBBIE FOWLER MADE IT 4-3 IN THE DYING MOMENTS.
THE FIRST OF MANY..?
EVANS INTRODUCED A YOUNG MICHAEL OWEN TO THE FIRST TEAM IN 1997, AND WATCHED HIM SCORE ON HIS DEBUT AT WIMBLEDON.
He won the League Cup in 1995 but that was the only trophy he brought back to Anfield

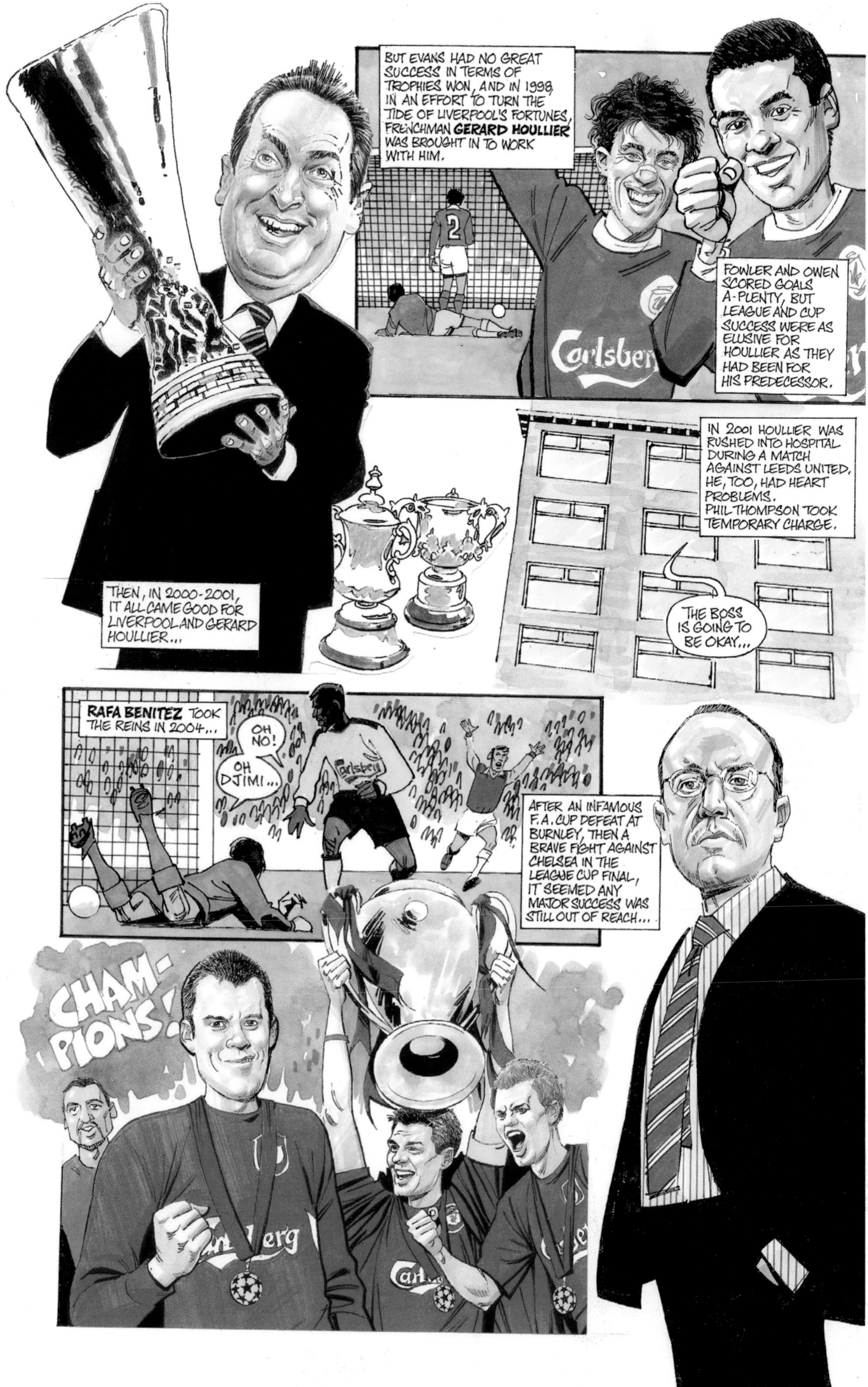
BUT EVANS HAD NO GREAT SUCCESS IN TERMS OF TROPHIES WON, AND IN 1998, IN AN EFFORT TO TURN THE TIDE OF LIVERPOOL'S FORTUNES, FRENCHMAN **GERARD HOULLIER** WAS BROUGHT IN TO WORK WITH HIM.
FOWLER AND OWEN SCORED GOALS A-PLENTY, BUT LEAGUE AND CUP SUCCESS WERE AS ELUSIVE FOR HOULLIER AS THEY HAD BEEN FOR HIS PREDECESSOR.
THEN, IN 2000-2001, IT ALL CAME GOOD FOR LIVERPOOL AND GERARD HOULLIER...
IN 2001 HOULLIER WAS RUSHED INTO HOSPITAL DURING A MATCH AGAINST LEEDS UNITED. HE, TOO, HAD HEART PROBLEMS. PHIL THOMPSON TOOK TEMPORARY CHARGE.
THE BOSS IS GOING TO BE OKAY...
RAFA BENITEZ TOOK THE REINS IN 2004...
OH NO!
OH DJIMI...
AFTER AN INFAMOUS F.A. CUP DEFEAT AT BURNLEY, THEN A BRAVE FIGHT AGAINST CHELSEA IN THE LEAGUE CUP FINAL, IT SEEMED ANY MAJOR SUCCESS WAS STILL OUT OF REACH...
CHAMPIONS!

CHELSEA GET THE BLUES...

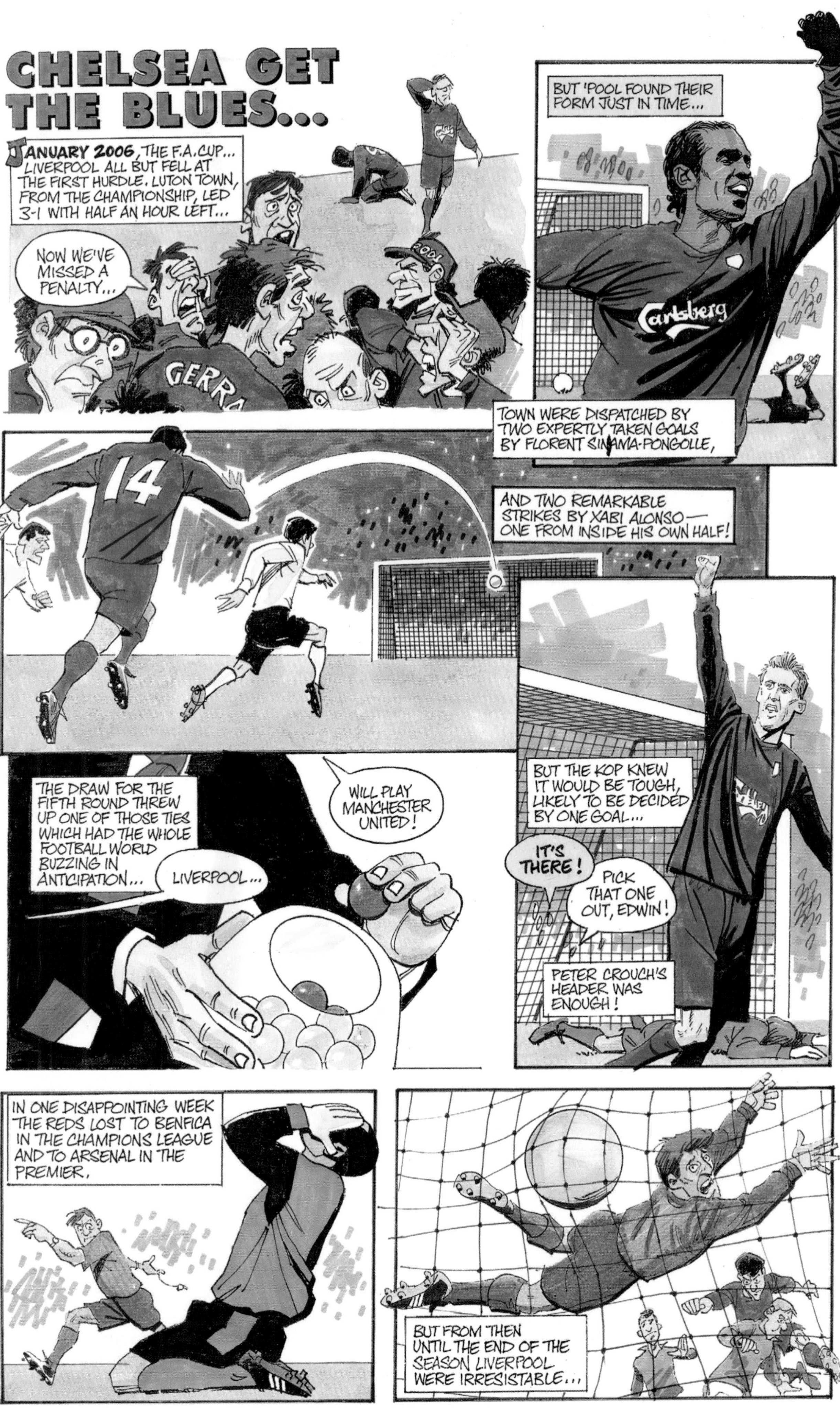
JANUARY 2006, THE F.A. CUP... LIVERPOOL ALL BUT FELL AT THE FIRST HURDLE. LUTON TOWN, FROM THE CHAMPIONSHIP, LED 3-1 WITH HALF AN HOUR LEFT...
NOW WE'VE MISSED A PENALTY...
GERRA
BUT 'POOL FOUND THEIR FORM JUST IN TIME...
Carlsberg
TOWN WERE DISPATCHED BY TWO EXPERTLY TAKEN GOALS BY FLORENT SINAMA-PONGOLLE,
14
AND TWO REMARKABLE STRIKES BY XABI ALONSO— ONE FROM INSIDE HIS OWN HALF!
THE DRAW FOR THE FIFTH ROUND THREW UP ONE OF THOSE TIES WHICH HAD THE WHOLE FOOTBALL WORLD BUZZING IN ANTICIPATION...
LIVERPOOL...
WILL PLAY MANCHESTER UNITED!
BUT THE KOP KNEW IT WOULD BE TOUGH, LIKELY TO BE DECIDED BY ONE GOAL...
IT'S THERE!
PICK THAT ONE OUT, EDWIN!
PETER CROUCH'S HEADER WAS ENOUGH!
IN ONE DISAPPOINTING WEEK THE REDS LOST TO BENFICA IN THE CHAMPIONS LEAGUE AND TO ARSENAL IN THE PREMIER,
BUT FROM THEN UNTIL THE END OF THE SEASON LIVERPOOL WERE IRRESISTABLE...

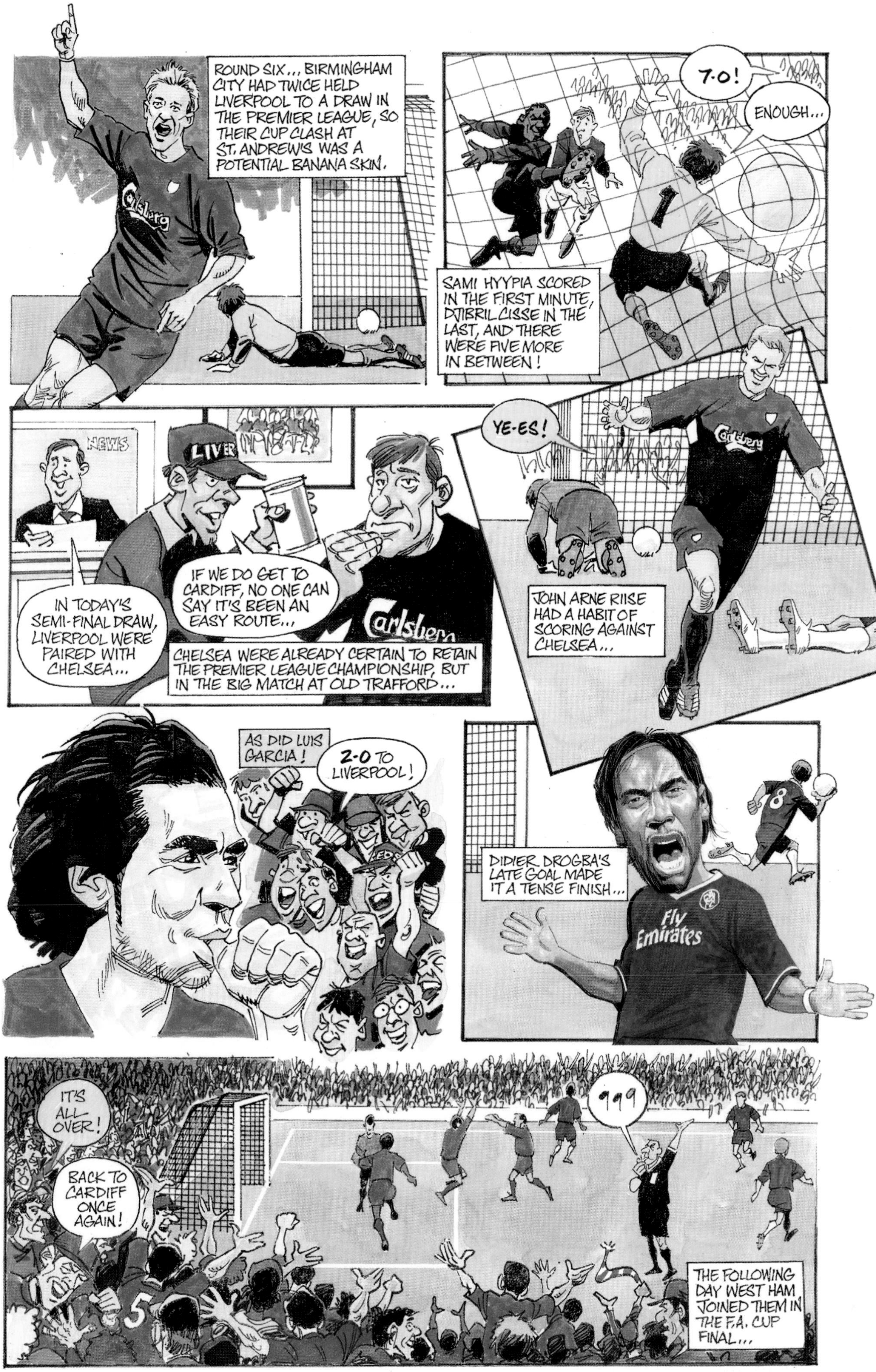
ROUND SIX... BIRMINGHAM CITY HAD TWICE HELD LIVERPOOL TO A DRAW IN THE PREMIER LEAGUE, SO THEIR CUP CLASH AT ST. ANDREW'S WAS A POTENTIAL BANANA SKIN.
7-0!
ENOUGH...
SAMI HYYPIA SCORED IN THE FIRST MINUTE, DJIBRIL CISSE IN THE LAST, AND THERE WERE FIVE MORE IN BETWEEN!
NEWS
LIVER
IN TODAY'S SEMI-FINAL DRAW, LIVERPOOL WERE PAIRED WITH CHELSEA...
IF WE DO GET TO CARDIFF, NO ONE CAN SAY IT'S BEEN AN EASY ROUTE...
CHELSEA WERE ALREADY CERTAIN TO RETAIN THE PREMIER LEAGUE CHAMPIONSHIP, BUT IN THE BIG MATCH AT OLD TRAFFORD...
YE-ES!
JOHN ARNE RIISE HAD A HABIT OF SCORING AGAINST CHELSEA...
AS DID LUIS GARCIA!
2-0 TO LIVERPOOL!
DIDIER DROGBA'S LATE GOAL MADE IT A TENSE FINISH...
Fly Emirates
IT'S ALL OVER!
BACK TO CARDIFF ONCE AGAIN!
THE FOLLOWING DAY WEST HAM JOINED THEM IN THE F.A. CUP FINAL...

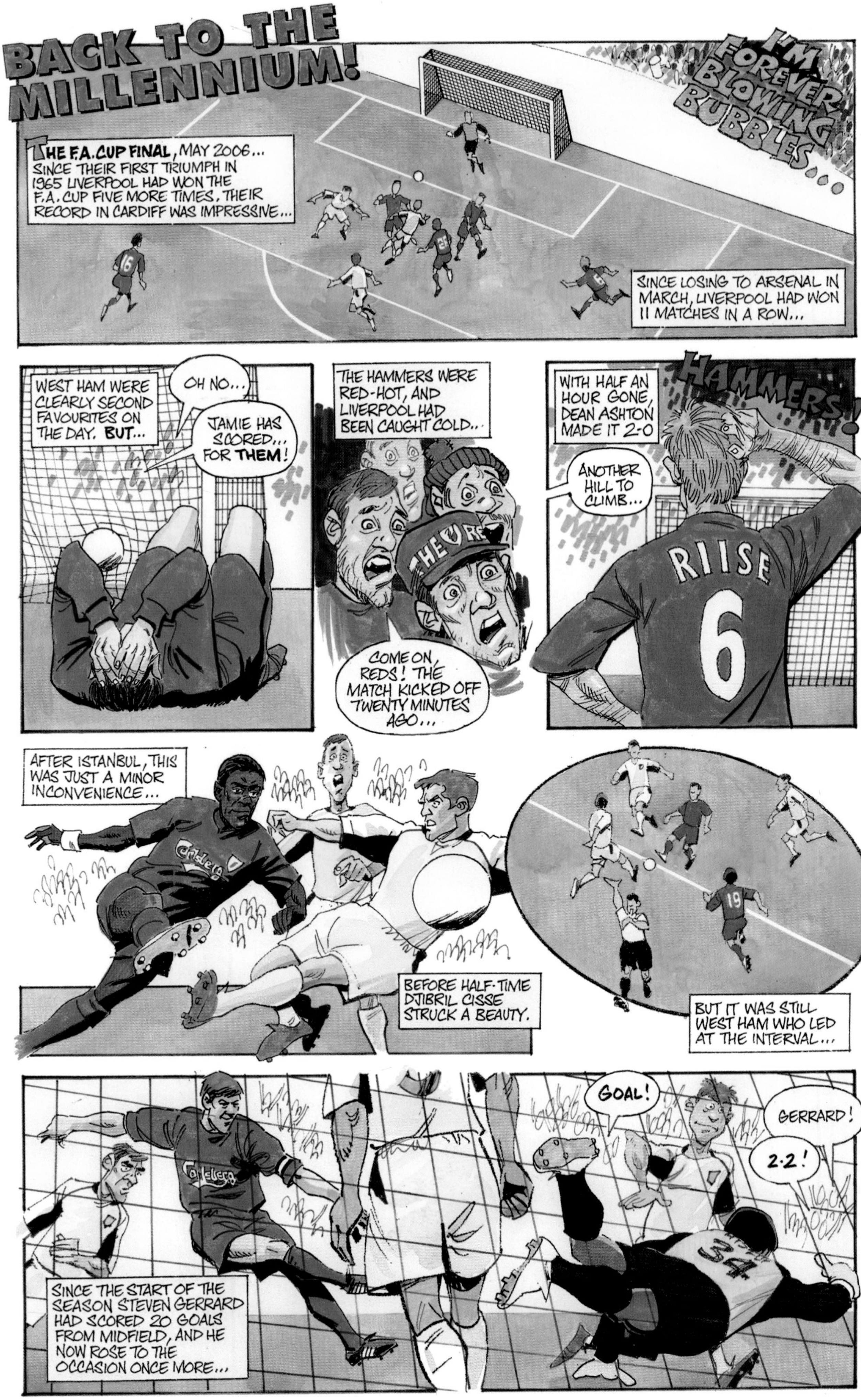
BACK TO THE MILLENNIUM!
THE F.A. CUP FINAL, MAY 2006... SINCE THEIR FIRST TRIUMPH IN 1965 LIVERPOOL HAD WON THE F.A. CUP FIVE MORE TIMES. THEIR RECORD IN CARDIFF WAS IMPRESSIVE...
I'M FOREVER BLOWING BUBBLES...
SINCE LOSING TO ARSENAL IN MARCH, LIVERPOOL HAD WON 11 MATCHES IN A ROW...
WEST HAM WERE CLEARLY SECOND FAVOURITES ON THE DAY. BUT...
OH NO...
JAMIE HAS SCORED... FOR THEM!
THE HAMMERS WERE RED-HOT, AND LIVERPOOL HAD BEEN CAUGHT COLD...
COME ON, REDS! THE MATCH KICKED OFF TWENTY MINUTES AGO...
WITH HALF AN HOUR GONE, DEAN ASHTON MADE IT 2-0
HAMMERS!
ANOTHER HILL TO CLIMB...
RIISE
6
AFTER ISTANBUL, THIS WAS JUST A MINOR INCONVENIENCE...
BEFORE HALF-TIME DJIBRIL CISSE STRUCK A BEAUTY.
BUT IT WAS STILL WEST HAM WHO LED AT THE INTERVAL...
SINCE THE START OF THE SEASON STEVEN GERRARD HAD SCORED 20 GOALS FROM MIDFIELD, AND HE NOW ROSE TO THE OCCASION ONCE MORE...
GOAL!
GERRARD!
2-2!

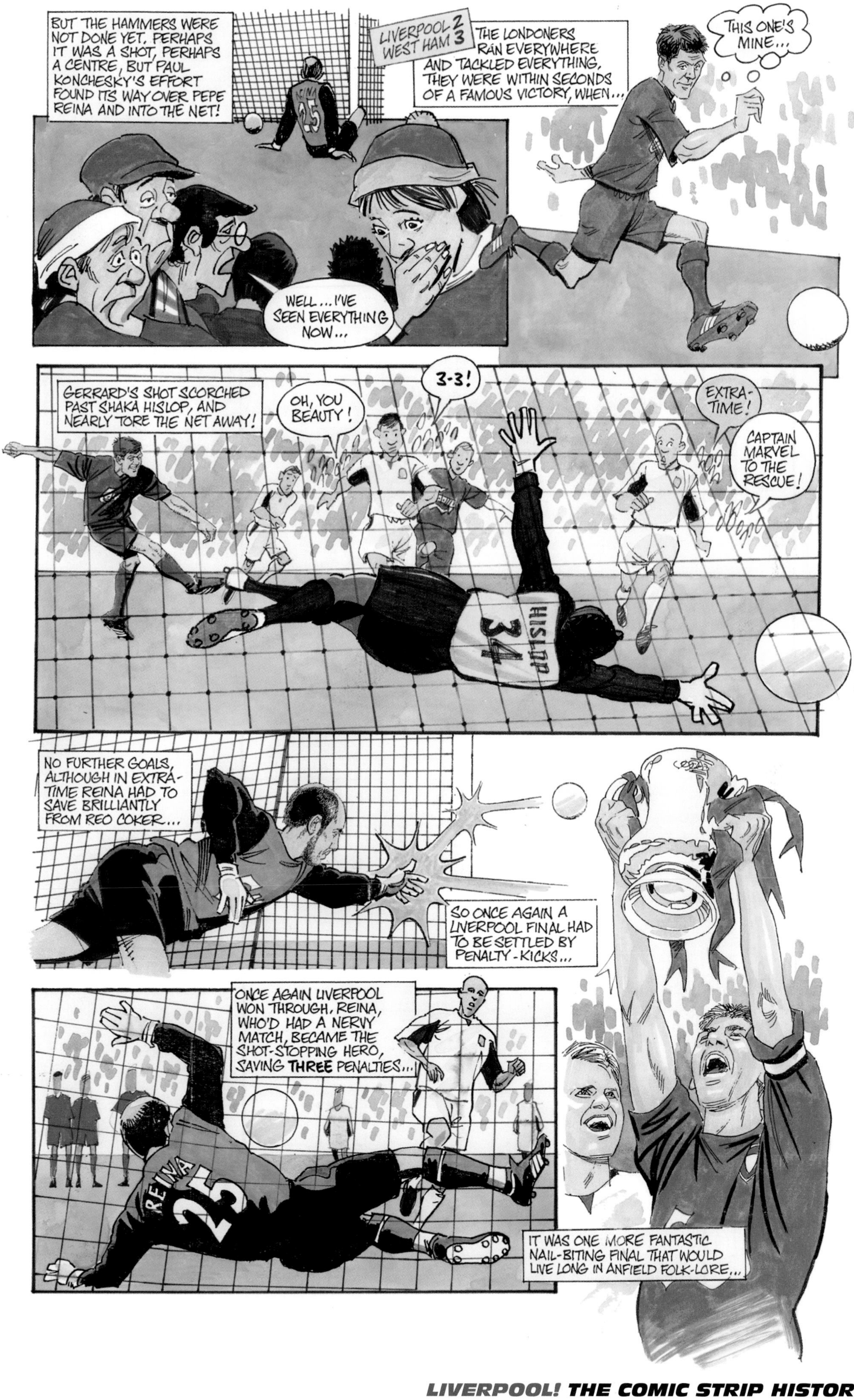
BUT THE HAMMERS WERE NOT DONE YET. PERHAPS IT WAS A SHOT, PERHAPS A CENTRE, BUT PAUL KONCHESKY'S EFFORT FOUND ITS WAY OVER PEPE REINA AND INTO THE NET!
LIVERPOOL 2 WEST HAM 3
THE LONDONERS RAN EVERYWHERE AND TACKLED EVERYTHING, THEY WERE WITHIN SECONDS OF A FAMOUS VICTORY, WHEN...
THIS ONE'S MINE...
WELL... I'VE SEEN EVERYTHING NOW...
GERRARD'S SHOT SCORCHED PAST SHAKA HISLOP, AND NEARLY TORE THE NET AWAY!
OH, YOU BEAUTY!
3-3!
EXTRA-TIME!
CAPTAIN MARVEL TO THE RESCUE!
HISLOP 34
NO FURTHER GOALS, ALTHOUGH IN EXTRA-TIME REINA HAD TO SAVE BRILLIANTLY FROM REO COKER...
SO ONCE AGAIN A LIVERPOOL FINAL HAD TO BE SETTLED BY PENALTY-KICKS...
ONCE AGAIN LIVERPOOL WON THROUGH. REINA, WHO'D HAD A NERVY MATCH, BECAME THE SHOT-STOPPING HERO, SAVING **THREE** PENALTIES...
REINA 25
IT WAS ONE MORE FANTASTIC NAIL-BITING FINAL THAT WOULD LIVE LONG IN ANFIELD FOLK-LORE...

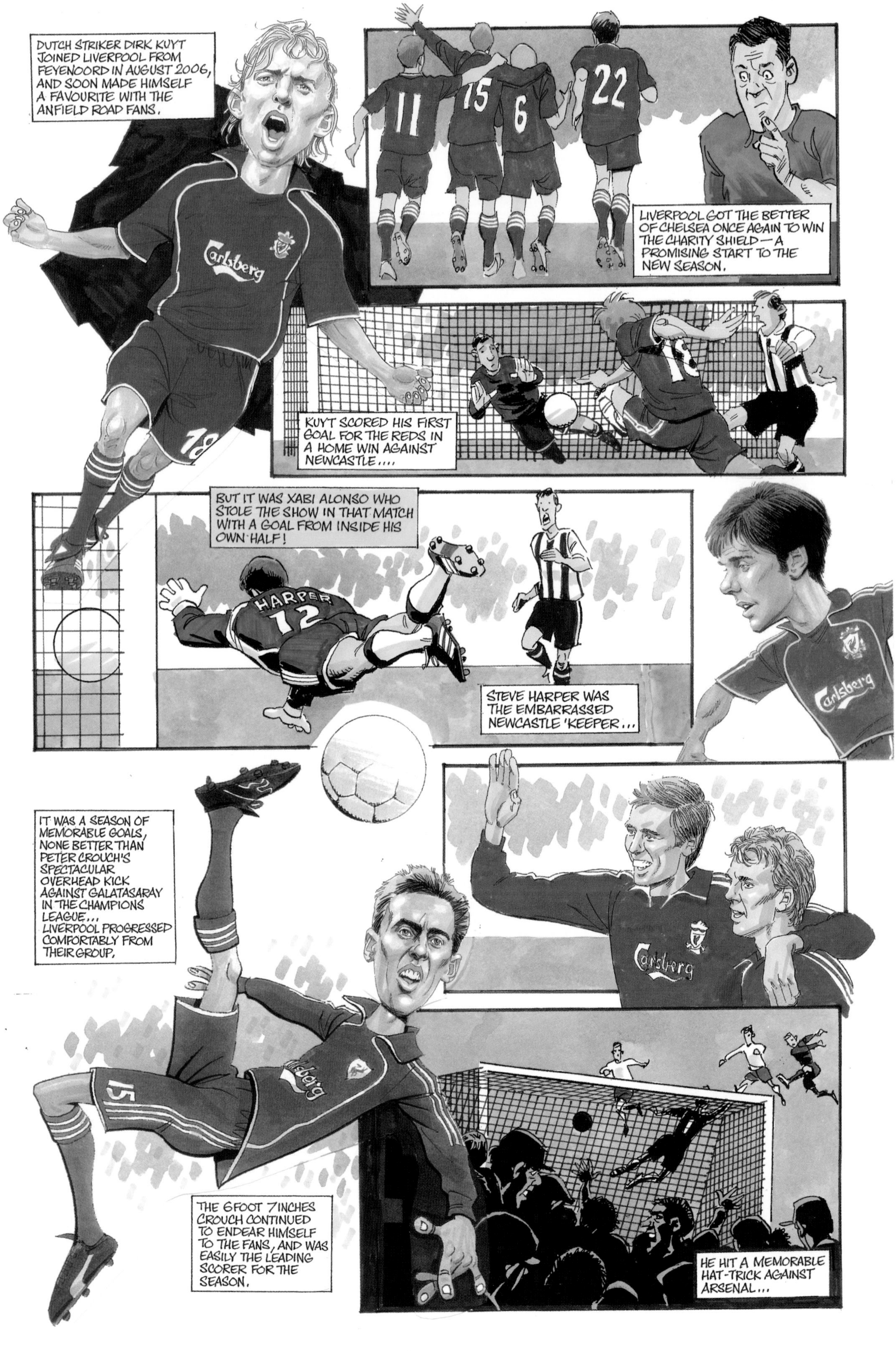
DUTCH STRIKER DIRK KUYT JOINED LIVERPOOL FROM FEYENOORD IN AUGUST 2006, AND SOON MADE HIMSELF A FAVOURITE WITH THE ANFIELD ROAD FANS.
LIVERPOOL GOT THE BETTER OF CHELSEA ONCE AGAIN TO WIN THE CHARITY SHIELD — A PROMISING START TO THE NEW SEASON.
KUYT SCORED HIS FIRST GOAL FOR THE REDS IN A HOME WIN AGAINST NEWCASTLE....
BUT IT WAS XABI ALONSO WHO STOLE THE SHOW IN THAT MATCH WITH A GOAL FROM INSIDE HIS OWN HALF!
HARPER 12
STEVE HARPER WAS THE EMBARRASSED NEWCASTLE 'KEEPER...
IT WAS A SEASON OF MEMORABLE GOALS, NONE BETTER THAN PETER CROUCH'S SPECTACULAR OVERHEAD KICK AGAINST GALATASARAY IN THE CHAMPIONS LEAGUE... LIVERPOOL PROGRESSED COMFORTABLY FROM THEIR GROUP.
THE 6 FOOT 7 INCHES CROUCH CONTINUED TO ENDEAR HIMSELF TO THE FANS, AND WAS EASILY THE LEADING SCORER FOR THE SEASON.
HE HIT A MEMORABLE HAT-TRICK AGAINST ARSENAL...

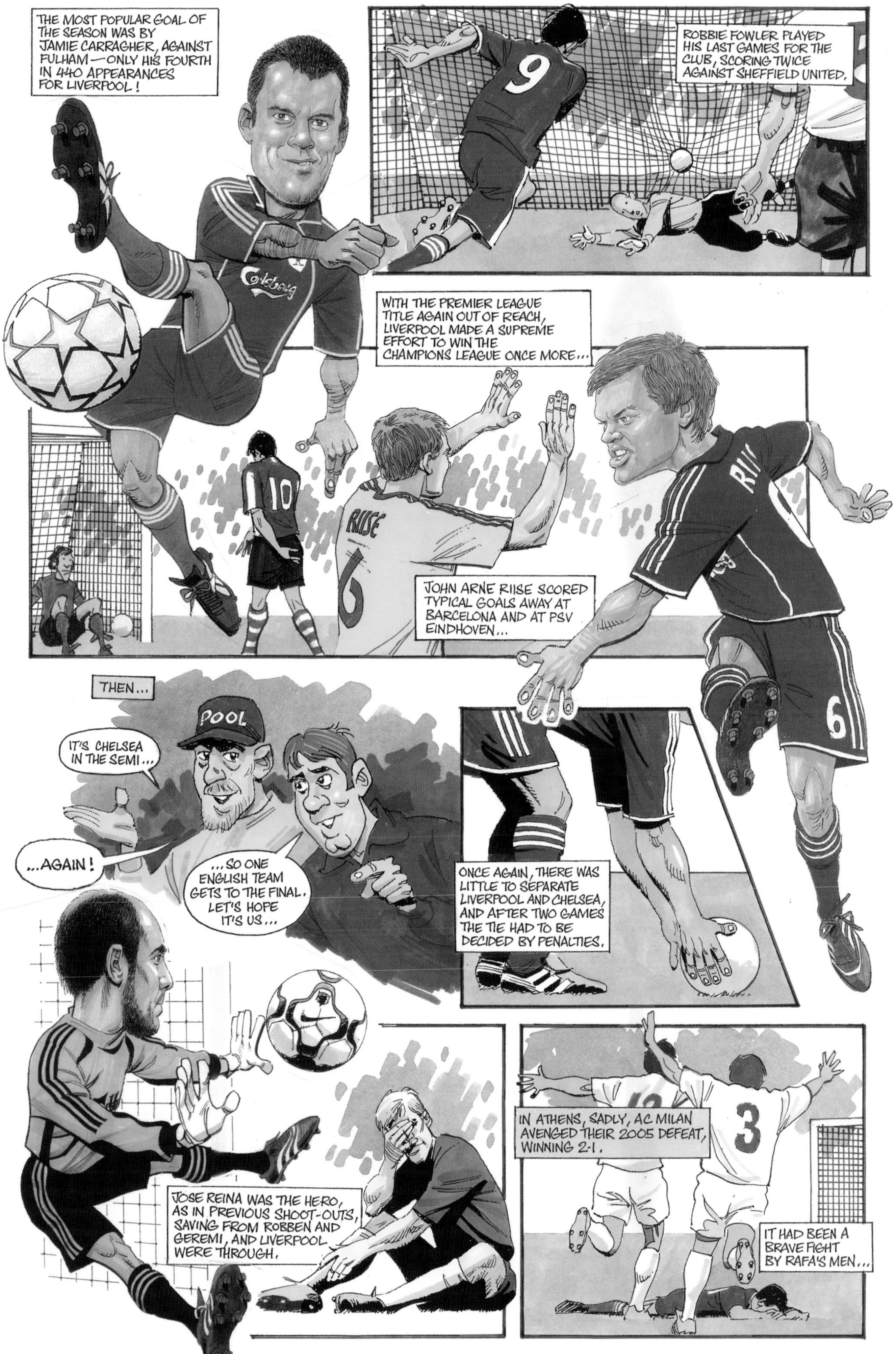
THE MOST POPULAR GOAL OF THE SEASON WAS BY JAMIE CARRAGHER, AGAINST FULHAM — ONLY HIS FOURTH IN 440 APPEARANCES FOR LIVERPOOL!
ROBBIE FOWLER PLAYED HIS LAST GAMES FOR THE CLUB, SCORING TWICE AGAINST SHEFFIELD UNITED.
WITH THE PREMIER LEAGUE TITLE AGAIN OUT OF REACH, LIVERPOOL MADE A SUPREME EFFORT TO WIN THE CHAMPIONS LEAGUE ONCE MORE...
JOHN ARNE RIISE SCORED TYPICAL GOALS AWAY AT BARCELONA AND AT PSV EINDHOVEN...
THEN...
IT'S CHELSEA IN THE SEMI...
...AGAIN!
...SO ONE ENGLISH TEAM GETS TO THE FINAL. LET'S HOPE IT'S US...
ONCE AGAIN, THERE WAS LITTLE TO SEPARATE LIVERPOOL AND CHELSEA, AND AFTER TWO GAMES THE TIE HAD TO BE DECIDED BY PENALTIES.
JOSE REINA WAS THE HERO, AS IN PREVIOUS SHOOT-OUTS, SAVING FROM ROBBEN AND GEREMI, AND LIVERPOOL WERE THROUGH.
IN ATHENS, SADLY, AC MILAN AVENGED THEIR 2005 DEFEAT, WINNING 2-1.
IT HAD BEEN A BRAVE FIGHT BY RAFA'S MEN...

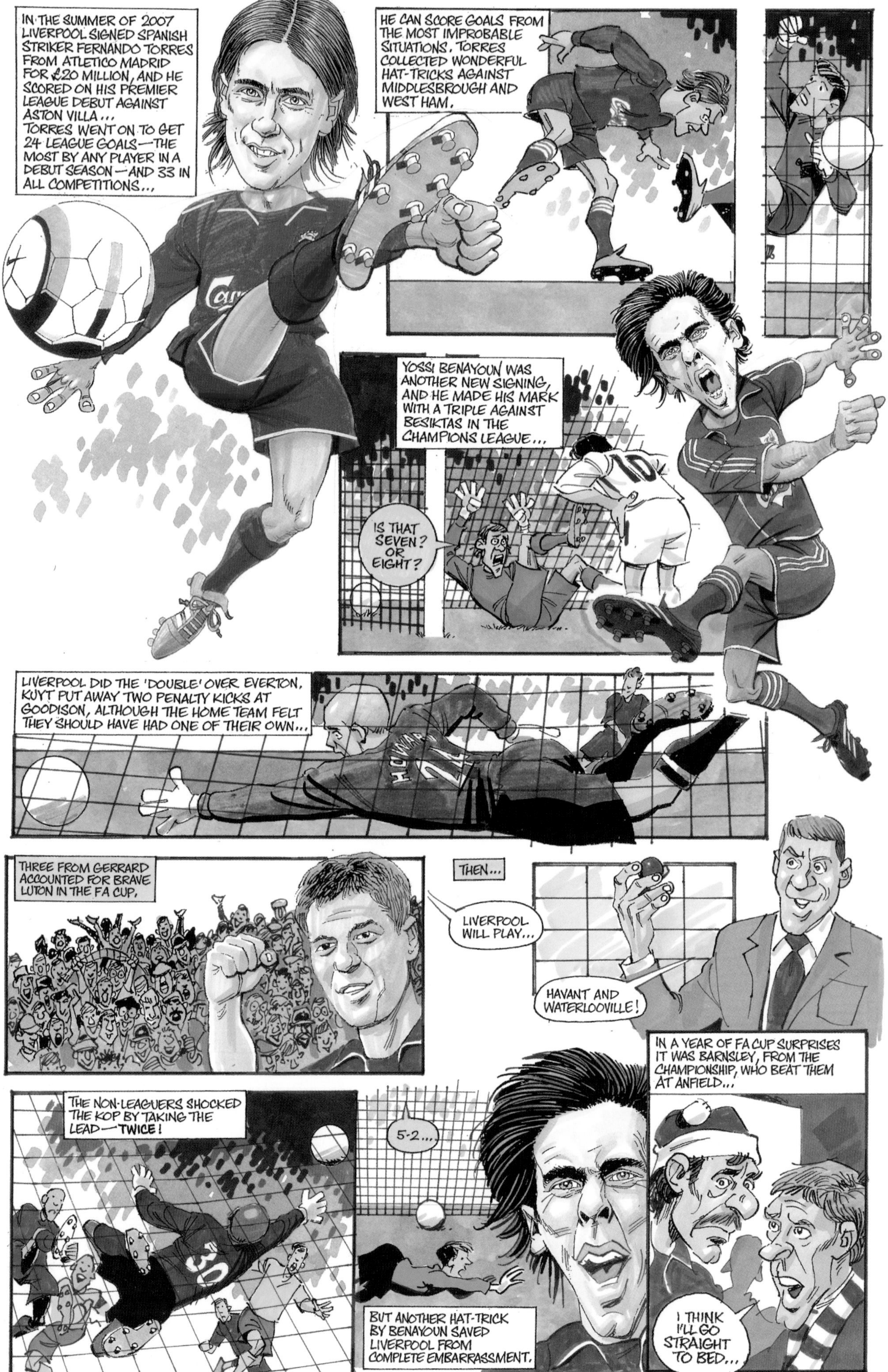
IN THE SUMMER OF 2007 LIVERPOOL SIGNED SPANISH STRIKER FERNANDO TORRES FROM ATLETICO MADRID FOR £20 MILLION, AND HE SCORED ON HIS PREMIER LEAGUE DEBUT AGAINST ASTON VILLA...
TORRES WENT ON TO GET 24 LEAGUE GOALS — THE MOST BY ANY PLAYER IN A DEBUT SEASON — AND 33 IN ALL COMPETITIONS...
HE CAN SCORE GOALS FROM THE MOST IMPROBABLE SITUATIONS. TORRES COLLECTED WONDERFUL HAT-TRICKS AGAINST MIDDLESBROUGH AND WEST HAM.
YOSSI BENAYOUN WAS ANOTHER NEW SIGNING, AND HE MADE HIS MARK WITH A TRIPLE AGAINST BESIKTAS IN THE CHAMPIONS LEAGUE...
IS THAT SEVEN? OR EIGHT?
LIVERPOOL DID THE 'DOUBLE' OVER EVERTON, KUYT PUT AWAY TWO PENALTY KICKS AT GOODISON, ALTHOUGH THE HOME TEAM FELT THEY SHOULD HAVE HAD ONE OF THEIR OWN...
THREE FROM GERRARD ACCOUNTED FOR BRAVE LUTON IN THE FA CUP,
THEN...
LIVERPOOL WILL PLAY...
HAVANT AND WATERLOOVILLE!
THE NON-LEAGUERS SHOCKED THE KOP BY TAKING THE LEAD — TWICE!
5-2...
BUT ANOTHER HAT-TRICK BY BENAYOUN SAVED LIVERPOOL FROM COMPLETE EMBARRASSMENT.
IN A YEAR OF FA CUP SURPRISES IT WAS BARNSLEY, FROM THE CHAMPIONSHIP, WHO BEAT THEM AT ANFIELD...
I THINK I'LL GO STRAIGHT TO BED...

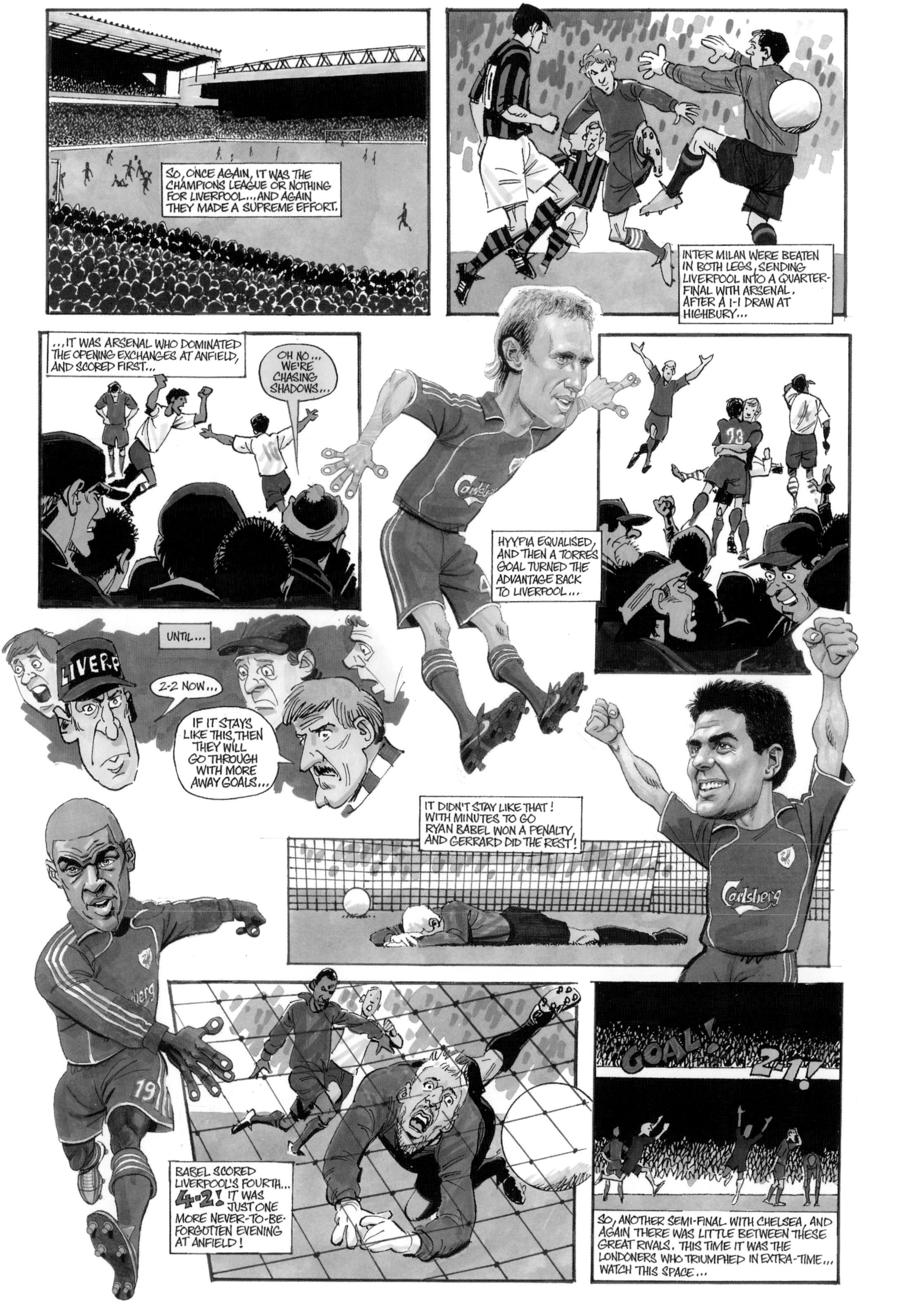

SO, ONCE AGAIN, IT WAS THE CHAMPIONS LEAGUE OR NOTHING FOR LIVERPOOL..., AND AGAIN THEY MADE A SUPREME EFFORT.
INTER MILAN WERE BEATEN IN BOTH LEGS, SENDING LIVERPOOL INTO A QUARTER-FINAL WITH ARSENAL. AFTER A 1-1 DRAW AT HIGHBURY...
...IT WAS ARSENAL WHO DOMINATED THE OPENING EXCHANGES AT ANFIELD, AND SCORED FIRST...
OH NO... WE'RE CHASING SHADOWS...
HYYPIA EQUALISED, AND THEN A TORRES GOAL TURNED THE ADVANTAGE BACK TO LIVERPOOL...
UNTIL...
LIVERP
2-2 NOW...
IF IT STAYS LIKE THIS, THEN THEY WILL GO THROUGH WITH MORE AWAY GOALS...
IT DIDN'T STAY LIKE THAT! WITH MINUTES TO GO RYAN BABEL WON A PENALTY, AND GERRARD DID THE REST!
Carlsberg
BABEL SCORED LIVERPOOL'S FOURTH... 4-2! IT WAS JUST ONE MORE NEVER-TO-BE-FORGOTTEN EVENING AT ANFIELD!
GOAL! 2-1!
SO, ANOTHER SEMI-FINAL WITH CHELSEA, AND AGAIN THERE WAS LITTLE BETWEEN THESE GREAT RIVALS. THIS TIME IT WAS THE LONDONERS WHO TRIUMPHED IN EXTRA-TIME... WATCH THIS SPACE...

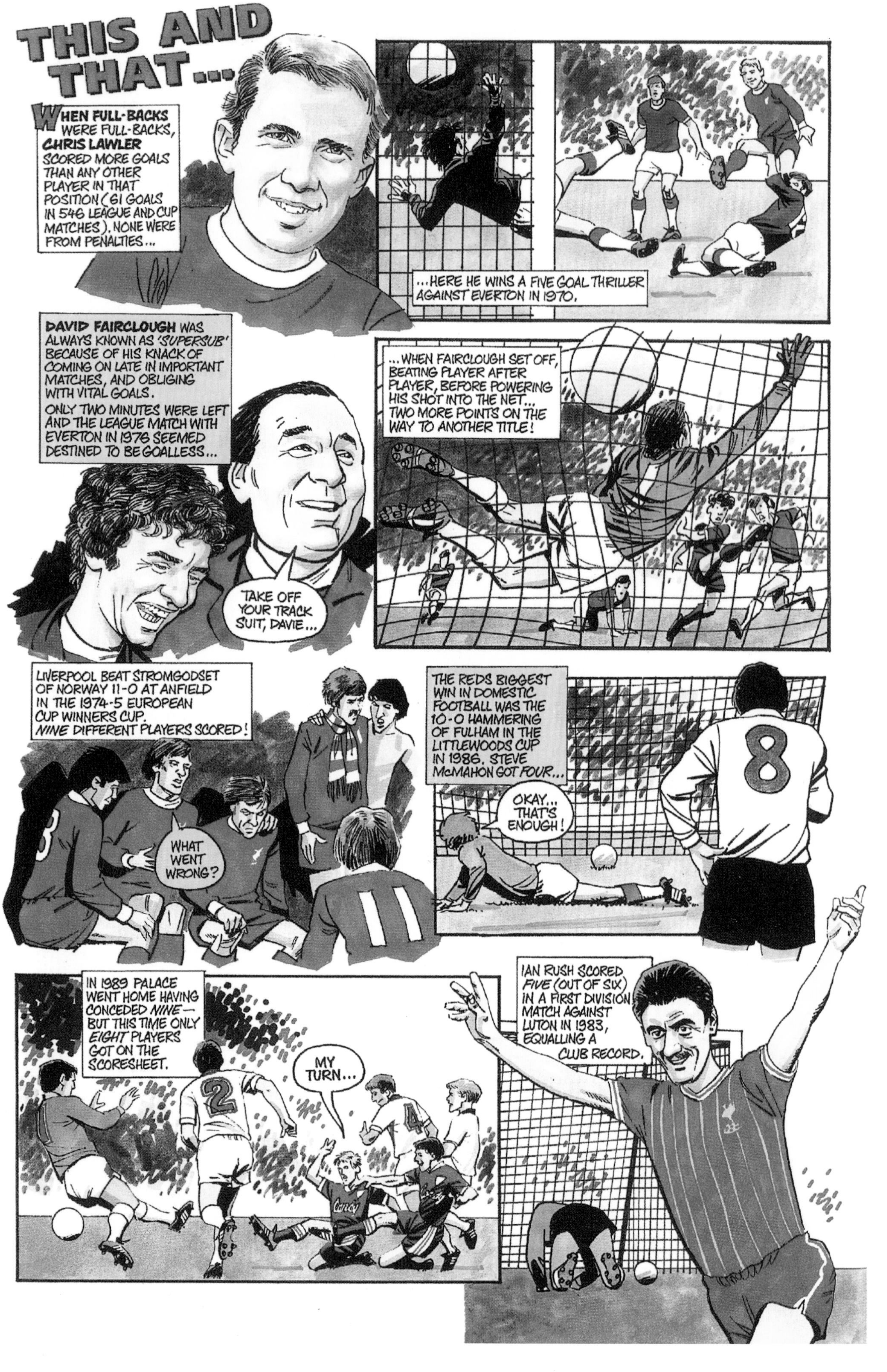
THIS AND THAT...
WHEN FULL-BACKS WERE FULL-BACKS, CHRIS LAWLER SCORED MORE GOALS THAN ANY OTHER PLAYER IN THAT POSITION (61 GOALS IN 546 LEAGUE AND CUP MATCHES). NONE WERE FROM PENALTIES...
...HERE HE WINS A FIVE GOAL THRILLER AGAINST EVERTON IN 1970.
DAVID FAIRCLOUGH WAS ALWAYS KNOWN AS 'SUPERSUB' BECAUSE OF HIS KNACK OF COMING ON LATE IN IMPORTANT MATCHES, AND OBLIGING WITH VITAL GOALS.
ONLY TWO MINUTES WERE LEFT AND THE LEAGUE MATCH WITH EVERTON IN 1976 SEEMED DESTINED TO BE GOALLESS...
TAKE OFF YOUR TRACK SUIT, DAVIE...
...WHEN FAIRCLOUGH SET OFF, BEATING PLAYER AFTER PLAYER, BEFORE POWERING HIS SHOT INTO THE NET... TWO MORE POINTS ON THE WAY TO ANOTHER TITLE!
LIVERPOOL BEAT STROMGODSET OF NORWAY 11-0 AT ANFIELD IN THE 1974-5 EUROPEAN CUP WINNERS CUP. NINE DIFFERENT PLAYERS SCORED!
WHAT WENT WRONG?
THE REDS BIGGEST WIN IN DOMESTIC FOOTBALL WAS THE 10-0 HAMMERING OF FULHAM IN THE LITTLEWOODS CUP IN 1986. STEVE McMAHON GOT FOUR...
OKAY... THAT'S ENOUGH!
IN 1989 PALACE WENT HOME HAVING CONCEDED NINE— BUT THIS TIME ONLY EIGHT PLAYERS GOT ON THE SCORESHEET.
MY TURN...
IAN RUSH SCORED FIVE (OUT OF SIX) IN A FIRST DIVISION MATCH AGAINST LUTON IN 1983, EQUALLING A CLUB RECORD.

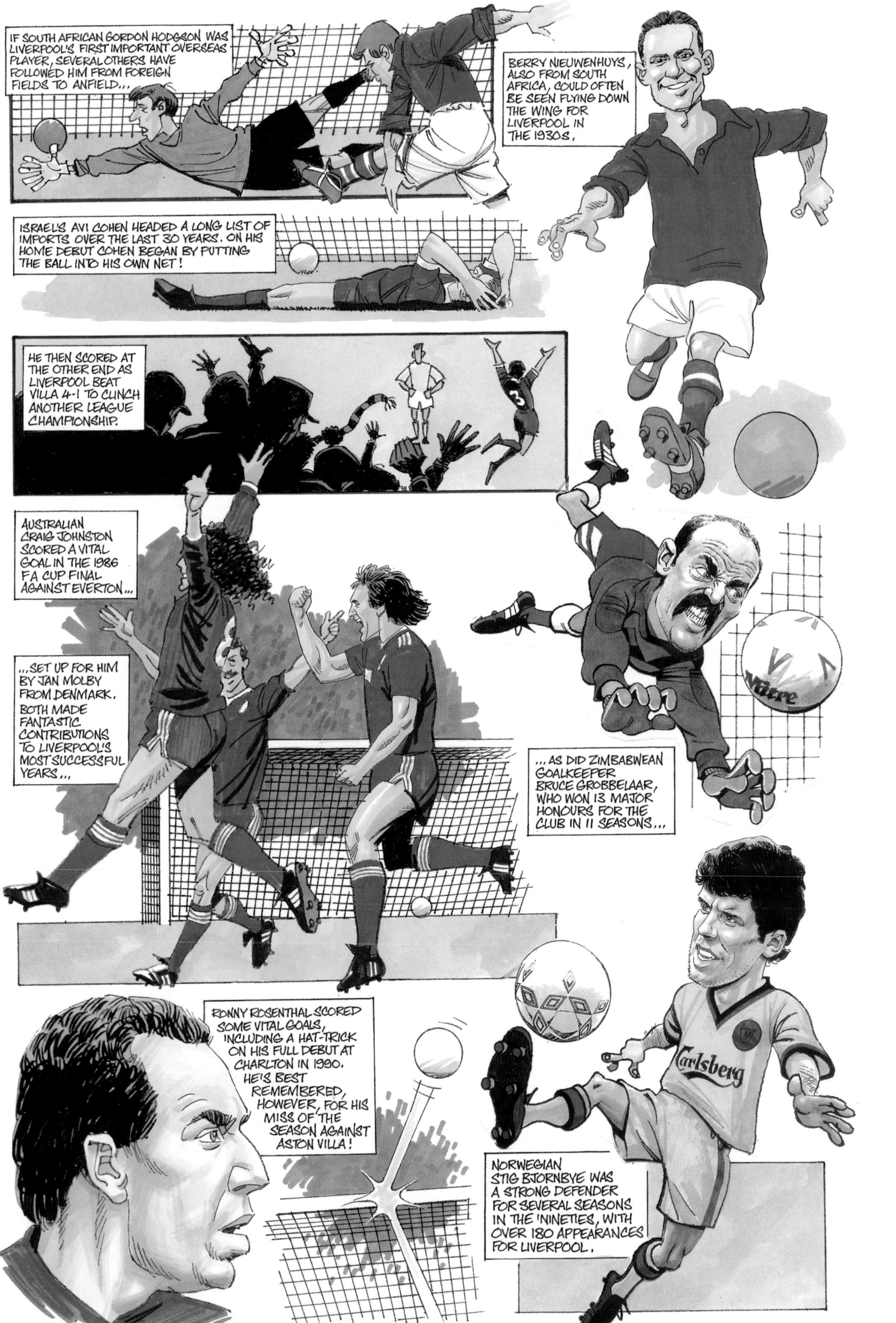
IF SOUTH AFRICAN GORDON HODGSON WAS LIVERPOOL'S FIRST IMPORTANT OVERSEAS PLAYER, SEVERAL OTHERS HAVE FOLLOWED HIM FROM FOREIGN FIELDS TO ANFIELD...
BERRY NIEUWENHUYS, ALSO FROM SOUTH AFRICA, COULD OFTEN BE SEEN FLYING DOWN THE WING FOR LIVERPOOL IN THE 1930S.
ISRAEL'S AVI COHEN HEADED A LONG LIST OF IMPORTS OVER THE LAST 30 YEARS. ON HIS HOME DEBUT COHEN BEGAN BY PUTTING THE BALL INTO HIS OWN NET!
HE THEN SCORED AT THE OTHER END AS LIVERPOOL BEAT VILLA 4-1 TO CLINCH ANOTHER LEAGUE CHAMPIONSHIP.
AUSTRALIAN CRAIG JOHNSTON SCORED A VITAL GOAL IN THE 1986 F.A. CUP FINAL AGAINST EVERTON...
...SET UP FOR HIM BY JAN MOLBY FROM DENMARK. BOTH MADE FANTASTIC CONTRIBUTIONS TO LIVERPOOL'S MOST SUCCESSFUL YEARS...
...AS DID ZIMBABWEAN GOALKEEPER BRUCE GROBBELAAR, WHO WON 13 MAJOR HONOURS FOR THE CLUB IN 11 SEASONS...
Mitre
RONNY ROSENTHAL SCORED SOME VITAL GOALS, INCLUDING A HAT-TRICK ON HIS FULL DEBUT AT CHARLTON IN 1990. HE'S BEST REMEMBERED, HOWEVER, FOR HIS MISS OF THE SEASON AGAINST ASTON VILLA!
Carlsberg
NORWEGIAN STIG BJORNBYE WAS A STRONG DEFENDER FOR SEVERAL SEASONS IN THE 'NINETIES, WITH OVER 180 APPEARANCES FOR LIVERPOOL.

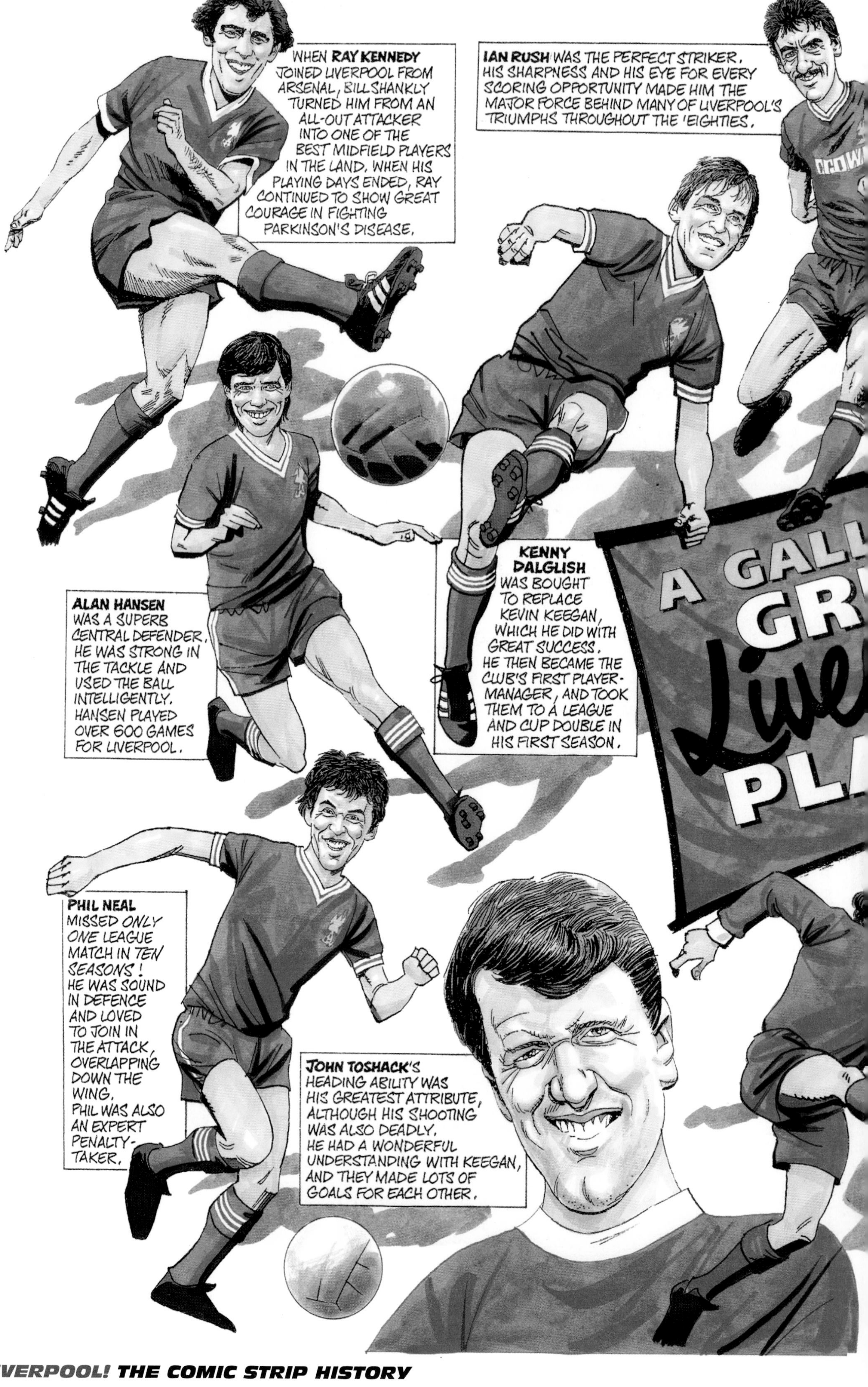
WHEN RAY KENNEDY JOINED LIVERPOOL FROM ARSENAL, BILL SHANKLY TURNED HIM FROM AN ALL-OUT ATTACKER INTO ONE OF THE BEST MIDFIELD PLAYERS IN THE LAND. WHEN HIS PLAYING DAYS ENDED, RAY CONTINUED TO SHOW GREAT COURAGE IN FIGHTING PARKINSON'S DISEASE.
IAN RUSH WAS THE PERFECT STRIKER. HIS SHARPNESS AND HIS EYE FOR EVERY SCORING OPPORTUNITY MADE HIM THE MAJOR FORCE BEHIND MANY OF LIVERPOOL'S TRIUMPHS THROUGHOUT THE 'EIGHTIES.
KENNY DALGLISH WAS BOUGHT TO REPLACE KEVIN KEEGAN, WHICH HE DID WITH GREAT SUCCESS. HE THEN BECAME THE CLUB'S FIRST PLAYER-MANAGER, AND TOOK THEM TO A LEAGUE AND CUP DOUBLE IN HIS FIRST SEASON.
ALAN HANSEN WAS A SUPERB CENTRAL DEFENDER. HE WAS STRONG IN THE TACKLE AND USED THE BALL INTELLIGENTLY. HANSEN PLAYED OVER 600 GAMES FOR LIVERPOOL.
A GALL
GR
Live
PLA
PHIL NEAL MISSED ONLY ONE LEAGUE MATCH IN TEN SEASONS! HE WAS SOUND IN DEFENCE AND LOVED TO JOIN IN THE ATTACK, OVERLAPPING DOWN THE WING. PHIL WAS ALSO AN EXPERT PENALTY-TAKER.
JOHN TOSHACK'S HEADING ABILITY WAS HIS GREATEST ATTRIBUTE, ALTHOUGH HIS SHOOTING WAS ALSO DEADLY. HE HAD A WONDERFUL UNDERSTANDING WITH KEEGAN, AND THEY MADE LOTS OF GOALS FOR EACH OTHER.

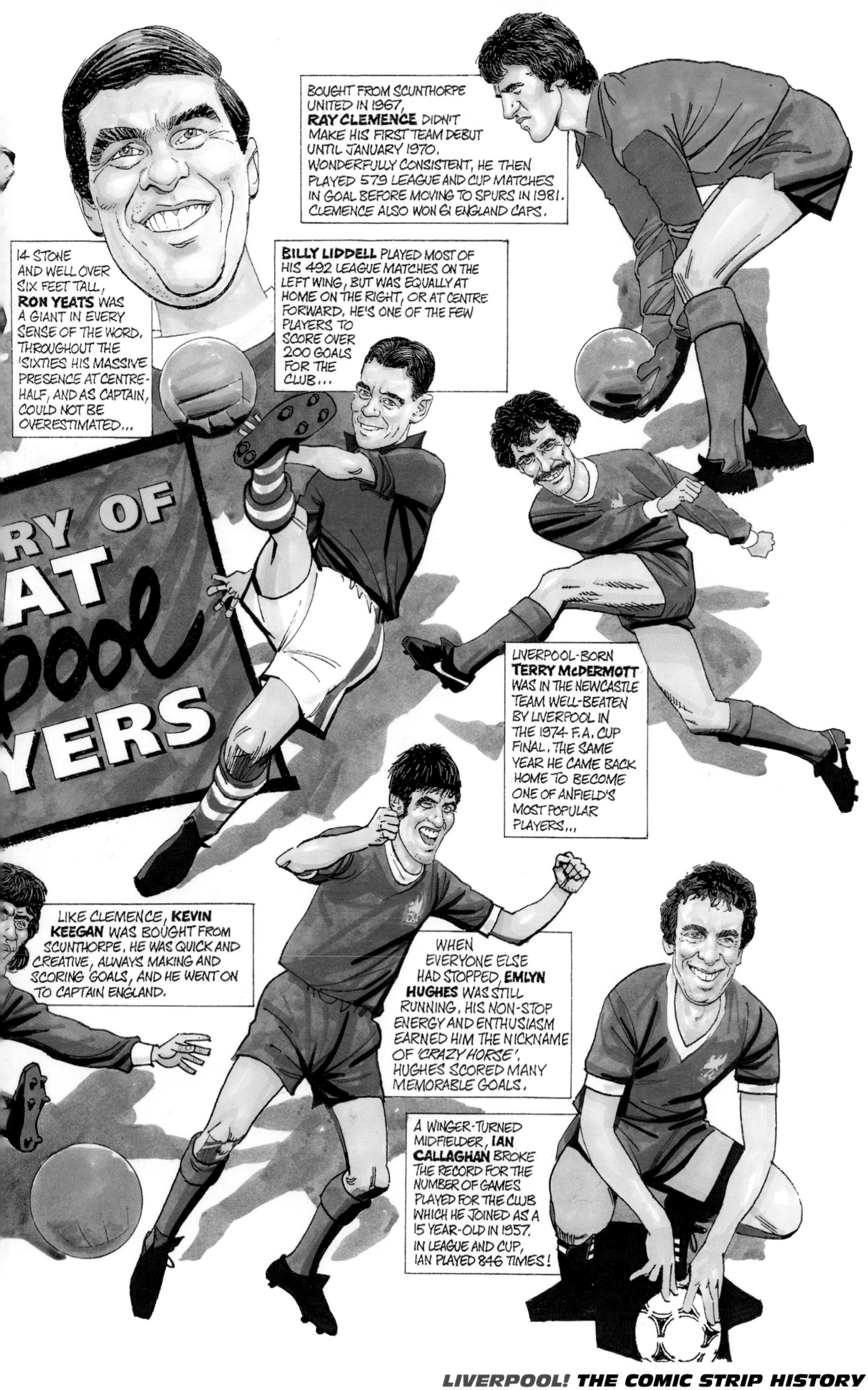
BOUGHT FROM SCUNTHORPE UNITED IN 1967, **RAY CLEMENCE** DIDN'T MAKE HIS FIRST TEAM DEBUT UNTIL JANUARY 1970. WONDERFULLY CONSISTENT, HE THEN PLAYED 579 LEAGUE AND CUP MATCHES IN GOAL BEFORE MOVING TO SPURS IN 1981. CLEMENCE ALSO WON 61 ENGLAND CAPS.
14 STONE AND WELL OVER SIX FEET TALL, **RON YEATS** WAS A GIANT IN EVERY SENSE OF THE WORD. THROUGHOUT THE 'SIXTIES HIS MASSIVE PRESENCE AT CENTRE-HALF, AND AS CAPTAIN, COULD NOT BE OVERESTIMATED...
BILLY LIDDELL PLAYED MOST OF HIS 492 LEAGUE MATCHES ON THE LEFT WING, BUT WAS EQUALLY AT HOME ON THE RIGHT, OR AT CENTRE FORWARD. HE'S ONE OF THE FEW PLAYERS TO SCORE OVER 200 GOALS FOR THE CLUB...
RY OF
AT
pool
YERS
LIVERPOOL-BORN **TERRY McDERMOTT** WAS IN THE NEWCASTLE TEAM WELL-BEATEN BY LIVERPOOL IN THE 1974 F.A. CUP FINAL. THE SAME YEAR HE CAME BACK HOME TO BECOME ONE OF ANFIELD'S MOST POPULAR PLAYERS...
LIKE CLEMENCE, **KEVIN KEEGAN** WAS BOUGHT FROM SCUNTHORPE. HE WAS QUICK AND CREATIVE, ALWAYS MAKING AND SCORING GOALS, AND HE WENT ON TO CAPTAIN ENGLAND.
WHEN EVERYONE ELSE HAD STOPPED, **EMLYN HUGHES** WAS STILL RUNNING. HIS NON-STOP ENERGY AND ENTHUSIASM EARNED HIM THE NICKNAME OF *'CRAZY HORSE'*. HUGHES SCORED MANY MEMORABLE GOALS.
A WINGER-TURNED MIDFIELDER, **IAN CALLAGHAN** BROKE THE RECORD FOR THE NUMBER OF GAMES PLAYED FOR THE CLUB WHICH HE JOINED AS A 15 YEAR-OLD IN 1957. IN LEAGUE AND CUP, IAN PLAYED 846 TIMES!

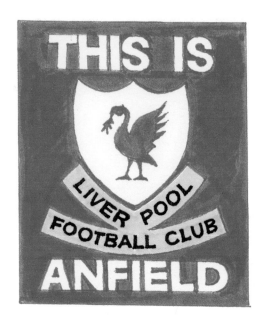

THIS IS
LIVERPOOL
FOOTBALL CLUB
ANFIELD

FACTS & FIGURES

HONOURS

First Division championship: 1900/01, 1905/06, 1921/22, 1922/23, 1946/47, 1963/64, 1965/66, 1972/73, 1975/76, 1976/77, 1978/79, 1979/80, 1981/82, 1982/83, 1983/84, 1985/86, 1987/88, 1989/90
Second Division championship: 1893/94, 1895/96, 1904/05, 1961/62
FA Cup: 1965, 1974, 1986, 1989, 1992, 2001, 2006
League Cup: 1981, 1982, 1983, 1984, 1995, 2001, 2003
Screen Sport Super Cup: 1986
Charity Shield/Community Shield: 1964*, 1965*, 1966, 1974, 1976, 1977*, 1980, 1982, 1986*, 1988, 1989, 1990*, 2001, 2006 (* joint winners)
European Cup/Champions League: 1977, 1978, 1981, 1984, 2005
Uefa Cup: 1973, 1976, 2001
Uefa Super Cup: 1977, 2001, 2005

All-time top appearance makers

1.	Ian Callaghan (1960-78)	857
2.	Ray Clemence (1967-81)	665
3.	Emlyn Hughes (1967-79)	665
4.	Ian Rush (1980-87 & 1988-96)	660
5.	Phil Neal (1974-85)	650
6.	Tommy Smith (1963-78)	638
7.	Bruce Grobbelaar (1981-94)	628
8.	Alan Hansen (1977-91)	620
9.	Chris Lawler (1963-75)	549
10.	Billy Liddell (1940-61)	534

All-time top goalscorers

1.	Ian Rush (1980-87 & 1988-96)	346
2.	Roger Hunt (1959-69)	286
3.	Gordon Hodgson (1926-36)	241
4.	Billy Liddell (1940-61)	228
5.	Robbie Fowler (1993-2001 & 2006-07)	183
6.	Kenny Dalglish (1977-90)	172
7.	Michael Owen (1997-2004)	158
8.	Harry Chambers (1915-28)	151
9.	Jack Parkinson (1903-14)	130
10.	Sam Raybould (1900-07)	128

RECORDS

Record win
11-0 v Stromsgodset (H), European Cup Winners Cup first round, first leg, 17th September 1974

Record defeat
1-9 v Birmingham City (A), Division Two, 11th December 1954

Carlsberg
8

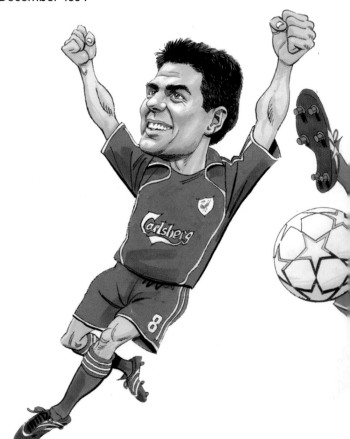

Most goals in a match by one player

5 John Miller v Fleetwood Rangers (H), Lancashire League, 3rd December 1892

5 Andy McGuigan v Stoke (H), Division One, 4th January 1902

5 John Evans v Bristol Rovers (H), Division Two, 15th September 1954

5 Ian Rush v Luton Town (H), Division One, 29th October 1983

5 Robbie Fowler v Fulham (H), League Cup, 5th October 1993

Most hat-tricks

17 Gordon Hodgson (1926-36)
16 Ian Rush (1980-86 & 1988-96)
12 Roger Hunt (1959-69)
10 Robbie Fowler (1993-2001 & 2006-07)
10 Michael Owen (1997-2004)

Most consecutive games played

1.	Phil Neal (1976-83)	417
2.	Ray Clemence (1972-78)	336
3.	Bruce Grobbelaar (1981-86)	317
4.	Chris Lawler (1965-71)	316
5.	David James (1994-98)	213

PREMIERSHIP RECORDS

Most Premiership appearances

1.	Jamie Carragher	360
2.	Steven Gerrard	302
3.	Sami Hyypia	302
4.	Robbie Fowler	266
5.	Steve McManaman	240

Leading Premiership goalscorers

1.	Robbie Fowler	128
2.	Michael Owen	118
3.	Steven Gerrard	55
4.	Ian Rush	45
5.	Steve McManaman	41

Milestone Premiership goals

Date	Goal	Scorer	Opponents
19/8/92	1	Mark Walters	Sheffield Utd (H)
4/1/94	100	Nigel Clough	Manchester Utd (H)
1/10/95	200	Robbie Fowler	Manchester Utd (A)
19/2/97	300	Stan Collymore	Leeds Utd (H)
24/10/98	400	Michael Owen	Nottingham Forest (H)
1/4/2000	500	Michael Owen	Coventry City (A)
8/12/01	600	Michael Owen	Middlesbrough (H)
26/4/03	700	Michael Owen	West Brom (A)
5/2/05	800	Milan Baros	Fulham (H)
1/1/07	900	Dirk Kuyt	Bolton (H)

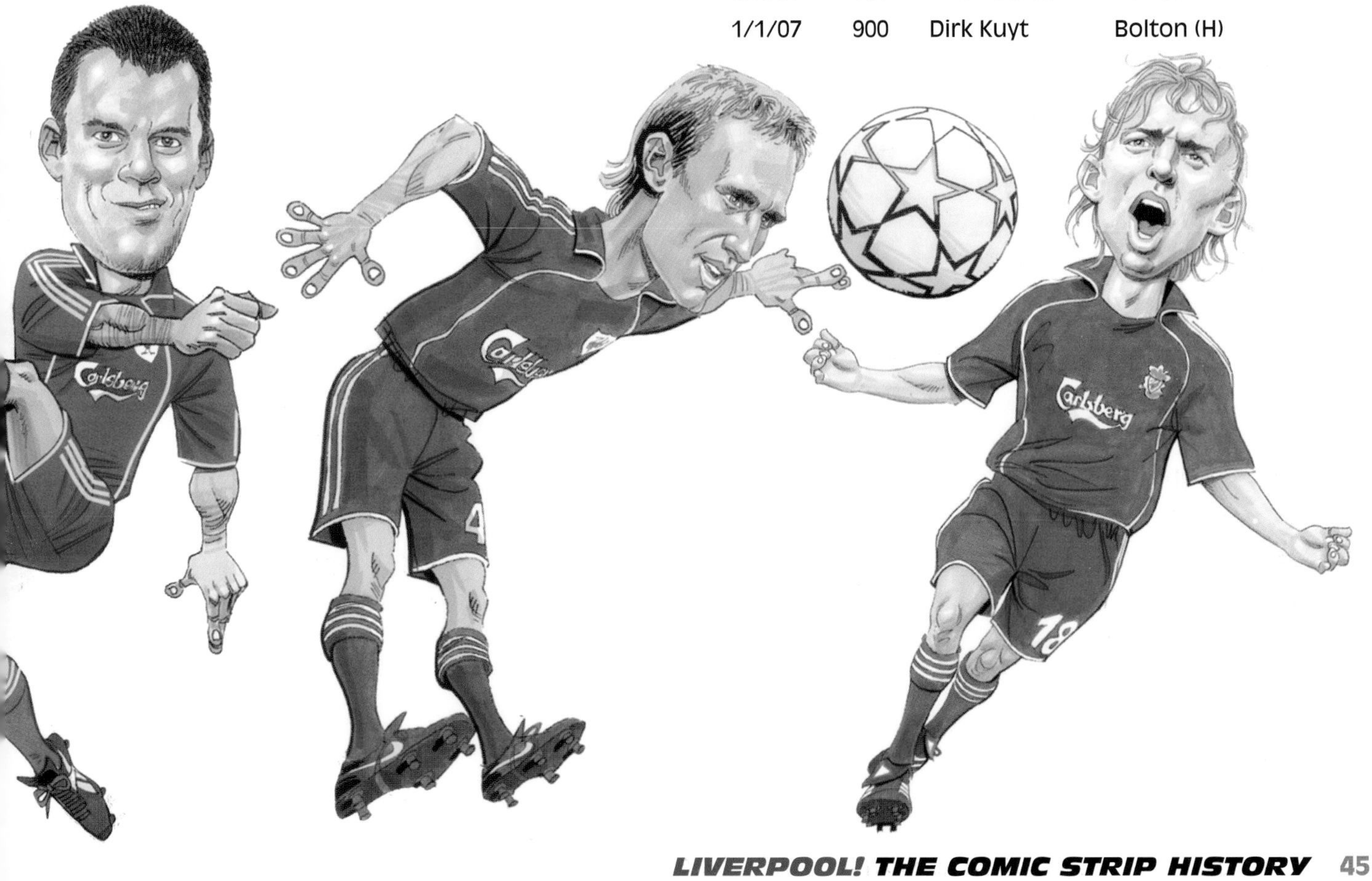
Carlsberg
Carlsberg
Carlsberg

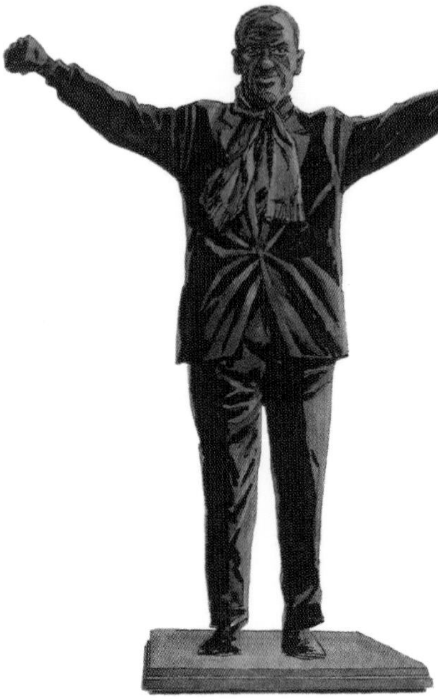

Published by Vision Sports Publishing 2008

Vision Sports Publishing
2 Coombe Gardens
London
SW20 0QU

www.visionsp.co.uk

ISBN 13: 978-1-905326-40-2

A CIP catalogue record for this book is available from the British Library.

Art and script: Bob Bond
Cover design: Neal Cobourne
Editor: Jim Drewett

Printed and bound in China by L-rex Printing Co. Ltd

Product Concept: **Ed Chatelier Edge Group**, The Creative Art and literary Group who originated the concept of Soccer Comic Histories including Liverpool, Man United, Newcastle, Everton etc. Also behind The Manga Bible (Hodders), Lion Graphic Bible (Lion) , Yun the Heavenly Man (Monarch) Godspeed Kurt Cobain Graphic Bio (Omnibus) and Terror rest Prayer (Highland Books) etc.

Contact **edgesword@yahoo.com** tel: 07905 060 775
www.edgeart.bravehost.com